GHOSTS OF TIMES PAST:

A ROADTRIP OF EASTERN OREGON GHOST TOWNS
2nd Edition

BY
KEITH F. MAY

PHOTOGRAPHY BY
CHRISTINA RAE MAY

Published by
Drigh Sighed Publications
327 S.E. 1st Street, Suite 131
Pendleton, OR 97801

D1732784

Published by Drigh Sighed Publications
327 SE 1st Street, Suite 131
Pendleton, OR 97801

Front Cover Photo of Store in Friend, OR
Back Cover Photo of Sparta Store by Christina Rae May
Illustrations by Keith F. May

First Edition
First Printing • 500 • January 1996
Second Edition
First Printing • 300 • February 1998
Second Printing • 300 • October 1998
Third Printing • 500 • October 2000
Library of Congress Catalog Card Number: 95-83484
ISBN 1-57502-107-2

Printed in the USA by

MORRIS PUBLISHING

3212 East Highway 30 • Kearney, NE 68847 • 1-800-650-7888

The drive,
the destination,
and the discovery
are all akin.

May you enjoy them as
much as we have.

The May Family

CONTENTS

North and South of the Wallowas

Other Ghost Towns in Eastern Oregon

More Stuff

FORWARD

In the first section of the book you'll look at the development of ten towns located in North Central Oregon. Refer to the map for specific locations. They can all be reached by paved road or by well maintained gravel roads (in the case of Friend and Lonerock). Allow yourself time to drive and enjoy the scenery. It is best if you take at least two days to see these towns.

Wheat, livestock and railroading played the major roles in the founding and development of these towns. Some towns were located at important crossroads or river crossings. Some were the product of two early railroads; The Great Southern Railroad and the Columbia Southern Railroad. Both railroads no longer exist, but were key factors in the settlement of the interior of the Columbia Plateau south of The Dalles.

Boyd, Dufur, and Friend were all located on the Great Southern Railroad, while Klondike, Kent, and Shaniko were built along the Columbia Southern Railroad. Sherrar's Bridge was an important river crossing on the Deschutes River, while Lonerock and Antelope were crossroads for freighters and stockmen. Ashwood alone, began as a mining town in this region.

In the next section of this book, you'll look at another region in Oregon where a railroad played a substantial role, along with gold and lumber, in the development of eleven towns in the Elkhorn region of Eastern Oregon. The narrow-gauge Sumpter Valley Railway no longer exists in the same form as it did at the turn of the century, but a section of rail and rolling stock are preserved for us to enjoy and admire as part of an era forever lost.

In the section titled "North and South of the Wallowa Mountains" you can take a look at five towns that developed on different sides of the same mountain range. Those on the south were developed around gold while those on the north were primarily agricultural in nature.

In the final section, there are nine more towns in various locations for you to explore in Eastern Oregon.

Ghost towns are the keepers of our past. They hold physical reminders of life as it used to be. Each town has its own character and personality to be explored and appreciated before they are lost to the ravages of time. Many of the towns in this road trip are still inhabited. Please remember to respect the privacy and private property of the residents.

WHAT IS A GHOST TOWN?

The term "Ghost town" brings to mind any number of images that include tumbleweeds, dust, and maybe even a few ghosts. These images have been promoted by Hollywood movies and dime store westerns. Just what defines a ghost town?

Some ghost towns still have lots of life in them, though nothing to compare with what they once were like. (Like Boyd, Flora or Lonerock.)

Some may even have a bright future, yet hold on to parts of the past with remnants lingering at every corner and may even have crowds of people at times. (Like Sumpter, perhaps.)

Some have never really died, but are drastically smaller than before; able to hold onto a post office, a store or two, and maybe a restaurant. (Like Shaniko or Granite.)

Some are a shadowy likeness of their past glory. Little remains to show what was once there. (Like Friend, McEwen, Cornucopia or Greenhorn.)

Some are dead and gone, with little or nothing left to remind you of a town. (Like Klondike, Auburn or Narrows.)

What is a ghost town, then? All of the above. Ghost towns can be categorized in several ways; by past and present populations, remaining number of buildings, age, industry, etc. Let's look at one particular way to categorize them: by "stage of development".

STAGES OF DEVELOPMENT

STAGE 1 DEVELOPMENT:

The town is established. Perhaps it has a post office, perhaps not. The buildings are mostly temporary in nature like tents, lean-to, or log cabins. Streets are dirt and may or may not be platted. No water systems exist.

STAGE 2 DEVELOPMENT:

The town has no tent structures. There are mostly log cabins, lean-tos and some frame buildings. Streets are platted and boundary lines are established. There is a post office. A water system may or may not exist. Streets are dirt but there may be board walks. Public structures are mostly wood frame with a few brick or stone buildings.

STAGE 3 DEVELOPMENT:

The town has few or no log cabins. Most homes are frame buildings. Most businesses are false front buildings. Some buildings may be made of brick or stone. The streets in the town are platted and lots in the blocks subdivided. Streets are maintained, either graded or plank. Most public structures, such as school and churches are brick or stone or at least elaborately decorated wood frame. Water and perhaps sewer systems would be in place. Telephone service would likely be available.

STAGE 4 DEVELOPMENT:

This town would be a strong mixture of frame, brick or stone residential homes. Most all major businesses and public structures would be brick or stone, with perhaps a few frame in-fill structures. Streets would be cobbled, plank, or macadamized. Water and sewer systems would be in place. Electricity and telephone service would be in place and available to most sections of the city.

Lets see how the towns from these two regions measure up. What stage of development did the town attain PRIOR to its decline?

TOWN	STAGE OF DEVELOPMENT
Albee	2
Antelope	2
Ashwood	2
Auburn	1
Bourne	2
Boyd	2
Cornucopia	2
Flora	2

Friend	2
Galena	2
Granite	2
Greenhorn	2
Kent	3
Klondike	2
Lonerock	2
McEwen	2
Paradise	2
Pine	2
Pocahontas	1
Shaniko	3
Sherar's Bridge	2
Sparta	2
Sumpter	4
Susanville	2
Whitney	2
Wingville	1

By looking at the list you can see that the majority of ghost towns listed only attained a stage two development. With little invested in the town, it appears that it was quite easy to vacate the buildings and move on to "greener" pastures. Sumpter, Kent, and Shaniko, on the other hand, had major development and population, perhaps making it more difficult to totally abandon the town.

Auburn, with the least development, reverted to nature the quickest, with nothing left but a cemetery as a reminder of such a large town. Klondike's only remaining buildings are the grain elevators and the brick school house while wooden structures no longer exist.

Antelope, Lonerock, Boyd, Ashwood, and Granite all reached a stage two development before going into decline. Yet all five maintain a year round population and have stabilized to some extent, perhaps even showing some growth over the past few years.

The only totally "un-populated" towns from this group are those of Friend, Flora, Promise, Cornucopia, Sherar's Bridge, Sparta and Whitney. (With the exclusion of nearby ranchers or farmers.) All had attained a stage two development, yet no longer sustain a regular population or any businesses.

So what is a ghost town? It is a reminder of the past - a shadowy presence of long ago glory. It must be looked at in a case by case study. I'm sure there are parts of some inner-city areas that could be classified as "ghost towns" by some and conversely, some ghost towns that would be too crowded for others.

GHOST TOWN ETIQUETTE

"Buildings that last become museums of the past."

Souvenir hunting can be an exciting avocation but, not in the case of these ghost towns. If you should see some interesting item; wood, metal, or glass, - it is important that you leave it where you find it for others to enjoy. Many ghost towns have almost disappeared piece by piece. It is best if all visitors to ghost towns respect the "No Trespassing" and "Private Property" signs. Especially in the gold mining regions. No one wants to be mistaken as a claim jumper and have a rainstorm of bullets come down upon them!

If you want a "piece" of the ghost town, take a picture. The town will never be in better shape than when you see it. Time and weather are slowing taking the buildings down - so preserve the sights with your camera - and document something that may never pass this way again.

NORTH CENTRAL OREGON REGION

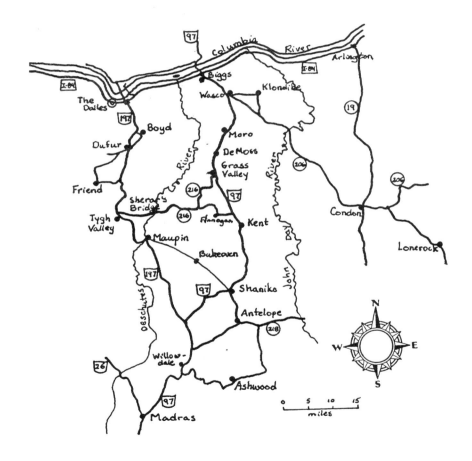

BOYD

The remains of Boyd can be found alongside State Highway 197 nine mile south of The Dalles. Fifteenmile Creek provided the stimulus for the small community. A good crossing of the creek had been established for travelers headed to the Barlow Trail and the gold fields of Eastern Oregon. By 1870, a store was located at the crossing. The town's name was in honor of T.P. Boyd, who settled in the area about 1883 and with his sons, had built and operated a gristmill and granary.

A town began to grow around the crossing and

A HOUSE IN BOYD

mill and on March 6, 1884, a post office was established with the name of "Boyd". Mr. G. H. Barnett, a local merchant, had suggested the name to honor the mill owner and the name was accepted by the postal authorities because it was both short and appropriate. Mr. John E. Barnett was the first postmaster.

Homes were built along the road leading to the creek crossing and the mill. Several are still standing and a few are still occupied. The homes were substantial for the era. Most of the community was built from 1884 to the turn of the century. The most outstanding buildings remaining are those of the mill (slated for demolition) and the three story rock home above the mill along with three or four homes in the old townsite.

The rock house was built by Mr. T. P. Boyd and it served as both residence and guest house for the customers of the mill. The home is still occupied and the water from the mill's holding pond is now used to irrigate the lawn and gardens.

The local wheat farmers used the mill's stone rollers to grind their wheat into flour which was then shipped into Dufur or The Dalles. The water-driven mill was technologically out-dated almost as soon as it was built. Most mills operating on electricity could process the grain quicker and for much less cost to the farmer. Shortly after the turn of the century, transportation by truck and rail, rather than mule drawn wagons, made a trip into The Dalles much easier. The decline of Boyd began when farmers started to go to the "big city" rather than staying in Boyd. Slowly the town lingered until the post office closed in the 1960's.

Recently, interest in Boyd has revived with the construction of new homes. With land use zoning laws favoring large tracts of land, the small parcels in the original townsite are attractive to people looking for a small acreage in the country to build on. The view of Mt. Hood and the wheat fields are spectacular. And what once was a day long trip to the "big city" in now a short commute down the highway.

A VIEW OF MT. HOOD

DUFUR

Though NOT a ghost town by any means, Dufur deserves a close look. It is the town that survived. It won out in the race to be a town of permanence in the wheat lands of Wasco County. In 1889, Dufur had a population of 500. In 1989, Dufur had a population of 500. Not much change in 100 years!

14 miles south of The Dalles on Highway 197 is this quiet, old town. Dufur has been a site of settlement since it's first settler, Lewis P. Henderson, arrived in 1852. Messrs. Reynolds, Marsh, and Brown established stock ranches nearby in 1855. And by 1863, David Imbler had built a farmhouse where Dufur now stands. In 1872, Andrew J. and E. Burnham Dufur bought a farm at the site of Dufur. A post office was established in 1878 and named "Dufur" in honor of the Dufur family. Chauncey A. Williams was the first postmaster.

Situated at a crossing of Fifteenmile Creek upstream from Boyd and on the route to the Barlow Trail, Dufur was just a small service site for travelers and local ranchers. Later, when the Great Southern Railway arrived in town, it became an important shipping center for the inland area of central Oregon.

Dufur is home to many fine old homes, century farms, and a fabulous little hotel that once served the passengers of the railroad: The Balch Hotel. It is located at the south end of town. Restored, refreshed and ready for travelers, this is the best place in the area to shake off the dust from traveling. Another site worth visiting is the log home of Joseph Schreiber, which houses the Dufur Historical Society. Dufur lives close to its roots. Wheat, cattle, and timber are what made Dufur succeed and continues to keep it going. Each August, the Dufur Threshing Bee recreates the old style wheat harvest chores using antique machines and old-time methods. Over 3000 people attend this annual event.

HISTORIC BALCH HOTEL - 1907

Dufur's claim to fame at one time wasn't wheat, but instead, apples! By 1916, the Dufur Orchard Company had planted 4,000 acres of dry-land apples and claimed to be the largest apple orchard in the world. Unfortunately for the company, apples need more moisture than the 12 inches of rainfall that Dufur averages a year. The orchards were pulled out, and wheat took over again.

Dufur almost became a boom town in 1908 when speculators claimed that oil could be found in the nearby hills. It took a local petition barring well-drilling to put a stop to the unfounded land rush.

Currently, Dufur is home to the Barlow Ranger Station which oversees 150,000 acres of the Mount Hood National Forest. A bank, pastime, grocery store, post office, hardware store, gas station and the Balch Hotel make up the rest of the businesses in town. Even though the railroad pulled up its tracks in the 1930's, Dufur has managed to maintain its claim of being a "real" town.

FRIEND

      Friend can be reached by driving to the south end of Dufur and turning right on Dufur Valley Road. After 1.7 miles, turn left onto Rail Hollow Road. The pavement will end after 2.5 miles, but the gravel road is in good shape. After 3.5 more miles a sign will point left to Friend. Another 1.5 miles will take you to a right turn and then 3.7 miles into Friend and paved road again.

ON THE WAY TO FRIEND

THE FRIEND STORE

     The End of the Line: that is Friend. The race for the railroads to reach into the center of Oregon had propelled the Great Southern Railroad Company into the interior south of the Columbia River. It reached Friend and went no farther.

     Friend was named for George J. Friend when the post office was established there in 1903 on his homestead. The first post master was Theo. H. Buskuhl. When the railroad finally reached Friend it enjoyed a boom town atmosphere for a short while. Goods, cattle, wool, and timber from central Oregon was brought to the rail terminus in Friend to be shipped to markets all over the world.

As the automobile age began to take over and cut into the profits of the railroad, Friend began to decline. When the Dalles-California Highway was built, engineers routed it miles away from Friend. When the railroad went bankrupt in the 1930's, Friend was left without an economic support and faded quickly into oblivion. The old school, a store, a few old farmsteads and the cemetery are all that remain to remind us of a once busy town.

The store, school and cemetery are about a mile apart along the paved road.

When leaving Friend, take the paved road east and it will return to State Highway 197 which is about nine miles away.

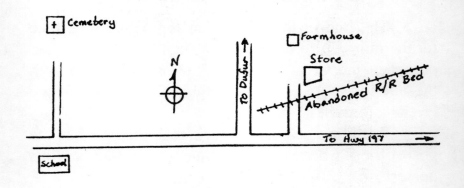

SHERAR'S BRIDGE

To get to Sherar's Bridge travel south on State Highway 197 to Tygh Valley. Turn left at the junction with Highway 216 and travel east. Four miles down the road is White River Falls Park. Be sure to take a rest break there and look over the magnificent falls and canyon. Sherar's Bridge is four more miles down in the Deschutes Canyon on Highway 216.

WHITE RIVER FALLS STATE PARK

Though not really a town, Sherar's Bridge was an important site in North Central Oregon. Located on the Deschutes River near the confluence with the White River, the site had been used as a fishing and river crossing site for centuries. Indian petroglyphs carved into the basalt cliffs near the highway are still visible though marred by recent graffiti "artists".

THE SITE OF SHERAR'S BRIDGE

Peter Skene Ogden visited the area in 1826 and used a bridge that the Native Americans had constructed. (He lost five horses that fell through the bridge.)

In 1860, John Y. Todd built a bridge, but it was lost in the flood of 1862 and had to be rebuilt. Later, Todd took in E.L. Hemingway and Robert Mays as partners. Hemmingway eventually bought out the other two and sold the bridge to a man named O'Brien, who in turn, sold out to Joseph Sherar in 1871.

Sherar paid $7,040 for the bridge and then spent $75,000 improving the roads leading to it. A post office was located at the site in 1868 with the name "Deschutes", but was later discontinued.

The upper country settlers preferred to use Sherar's Bridge instead of the bridge that was located at the mouth of the Deschutes River. With improved roads, packers and teamsters taking supplies to the John Day region began using Sherar's Bridge almost exclusively.

By 1893, Sherar had a well established clientele traveling through the area. He built the massive Sherar House at the west end of the bridge. It was three stories high and had 33 rooms. Miners, stockmen and freighters delighted in the tavern and the hot cooked meals prepared by Mrs. Sherar and her company of maids. Mr. Sherar would sit on the expansive front veranda and collect the bridge toll from travelers. In addition to the Sherar House and postal facility, the site had a store, livery stables and many other buildings. No trace of these buildings remain today.

In 1910 the railroad was built up the Deschutes River canyon. Large planks had to be laid on top of the Sherar House to protect it from flying rocks as the railbed was blasted out of the cliffs above. Once the railroad was completed, the freighting business all but disappeared and there was no more real business at the bridge crossing.

Mr. Sherar died in 1908 and Wasco and Sherman Counties purchased the bridge and eliminated the toll. The old bridge burned in 1940. A new bridge was built, but the highway alignment made it necessary to tear down the Sherar House to make room for the road. Mr. and Mrs. Sherar are buried in the Odd Fellows Cemetery in The Dalles.

WHITE RIVER CANYON

KENT

Kent can be reached from Biggs Junction by traveling south on Highway 97, or from Sherar's Bridge by crossing the bridge and following Highway 216 up the canyon walls for 11 miles after which a sign will point "KENT   13 MILES". The road will take you through the scanty ghost town of Flanagan.

Sixteen miles north of better-known Shaniko on Highway 97 lies the sleepy ghost town of Kent. In the era of expanding railroads, Kent became the terminus of the Columbia Southern Railway. For a short time, it was a boom town, until the line was pushed farther south to Shaniko.

A petition was circulated in 1887 for a post office to be located where the community now stands. The story goes that names were put in to a hat and a slip of paper with "Kent" written on it was pulled out. The community had a name.

Kent was a service town for the wide, dry Columbia Plateau region where stockmen and sheepherders roamed. It lasted well into the 1950's before falling into near extinction. The railroad came in 1899 and then pushed on to Shaniko. In 1936 passenger service ended on the railroad. In 1942 regular freight service ended on the railroad and the tracks were removed back to Kent. Kent's grain elevators then became the major source of income for the town. Irregular rail service came to remove the stored wheat down the line to Biggs Junction on the

Columbia River. The flood of 1964 washed out the tracks and the railroad was abandoned along with Kent.

NO GAS IN KENT

The community has an interesting collection of grain elevators, business buildings, church and a shell of a school, and several occupied homes.

The stone house is located across the street from the old service station on the main highway.

"MYSTERIOUS STONE BUILDING" IN KENT

A Mr. Wilson owned the house directly west of the stone building and the gas station on the opposite side of the highway. Electricity wasn't available in the county in the 1930's so Mr. Wilson built the stone igloo to house a generator that provided electricity to both his house and his gas station.

Since that time the stone building has been used for various other purposes such as a jail and a storm shelter. At one time there were wagon wheels attached to the front of the building, but they have long since disappeared.

One of the store fronts in "downtown" Kent has been placed on the Nation Register of Historic Places.

MAP OF KENT

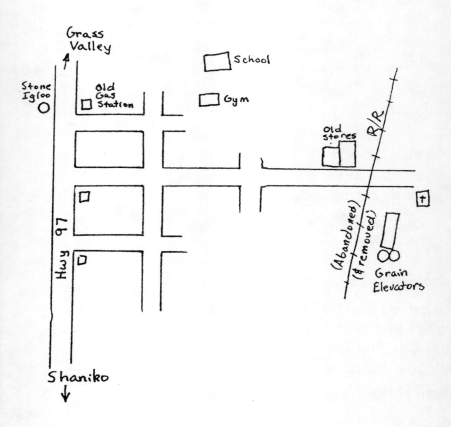

SHANIKO

Shaniko is a short 16 miles further south on Highway 97.

The unusual name of "Shaniko" is derived from the name of pioneer settler August Scherneckau. Native Americans in the area pronounced his name Shaniko, and the name stuck to the locality.

The Scherneckau ranch was on the stage route from The Dalles to Central Oregon. Mr. Scherneckau had bought the ranch from John and Elizabeth Ward in 1874 and operated the stage stop, saloon and 16 room inn at Cross Hollows, just south from present Shaniko. A post office opened at Cross Hollows with that name on May 23, 1879 and closed May 27, 1887. Mr. Scherneckau was the post master. Gustav Schmidt bought out Scherneckau in 1887 who then left for Astoria. The Cross Hollows post office ceased with the departure of Scherneckau. And with the establishment of the Shaniko post office on March 31, 1900, the Cross Hollows settlement formally ended.

The site for Shaniko had been selected for two major reasons: Water was available and the train tracks could go no farther south.

From the beginning, Shaniko was a planned town. Central Oregon of the late 1890's was sheep territory and the only outlet for the enormous quantity of wool being produced was The Dalles. Bankers and businessmen of The Dalles decided a rail line from

Biggs Junction on the Columbia into the center of Oregon could tap the vast market and increase their profits. The Columbia Southern Railroad was organized and construction began in 1898. The rail line reached its terminus in May of 1900.

SAMPLE
COLUMBIA SOUTHERN SCHEDULE
BIGGS TO SHANIKO
1900

Southbound Depart PM		Northbound Arrive AM
1:34	Biggs	11:25
2:14	Wasco	10:45
2:27	Klondike	10:30
2:45	Hay Canyon	10:15
3:00	DeMoss	10:00
3:09	Moro	9:50
3:44	Grass Valley	9:15
4:06	Bourbon	8:55
4:26	Kent	8:40
4:40	Wilcox	8:30
5:20	Shaniko	8:00

The town began as a tent city, but substantial buildings were quickly erected. Massive warehouses were built on the treeless plateau to store the bales of wool which by 1903 had sales of $3 million. By 1910, the town had a population of 600 and wool sales topped $5 million. Wooden sidewalks were extended throughout the town, and brick buildings were constructed such as the Shaniko Hotel.

THE SHANIKO HOTEL

The boom began to falter in 1911 when the Oregon Railroad and Navigation Company completed their railroad up the Deschutes River Canyon and tapped into the markets that the Columbia Southern Railroad and the Great Southern Railroad (terminus at Friend) had enjoyed. In the same year, an extensive fire swept through the town and destroyed most of the business district.

SHANIKO WATER TOWER

Businessmen in Shaniko managed to maintain their existence by hauling wheat from the interior, as the wool and stock markets began a long decline. In 1921, the first class graduated from the Shaniko High School. In 1925, The Dalles-California Highway was completed. Even though the highway went through Shaniko, it was a factor in the town's demise.

SHANIKO SCHOOL HOUSE

The highway allowed the trucking industry to begin hauling wheat to market cheaply. This took business away from the Columbia Southern Railroad Company, and in turn, decreased business in Shaniko. Gas stations came to Shaniko, but these couldn't replace the jobs lost in the warehouses and at the railroad. In 1934, the High School had its last graduation and in 1936, the railroad suspended passenger service.

By 1942, the railroad was in such decline that freight service was ended and the tracks were pulled back to Kent. The flood of 1964 washed out the train tracks to Biggs Junction and the railroad ceased existence altogether. By 1959, only 40 people lived in the town. Shaniko was designated as "Oregon's Ghost Town of the Year" (which came as a surprise to the residents!)

The grand old Shaniko Hotel became a group home for the elderly, and by 1977 was put on the auction block. It has undergone extensive restoration and operates as a Bed & Breakfast. Each room is named after a prominent historical person from Shaniko's past. The population has stabilized at about 30.

The many antique shops and interesting old buildings, such as the school house, water tower, and the hotel entice tourists to pull off the highway. Boardwalks still wander off into the grassy plains to nowhere, and the old railbed can be seen to the east. Residents are working together to preserve the buildings and old homes that have survived the dry, harsh climate of North Central Oregon.

Tales abound about the boom decade of 1900 to 1910. There are stories of an extensive red-light district that catered to both the railroad men and the sheepherders. Thirteen such "sporting houses" are reported to have operated at one time in town. In 1912, J.C. Fowlie, Mayor of Shaniko was assassinated in the streets of Shaniko. Tales of shoot-outs on Main Street between sheepherders and cattlemen were prevalent. Bootlegging was the major pastime during the prohibition era.

SHANIKO CITY HALL AND PARK

The Moody warehouses are mostly gone with one exception. Zenas Moody, former Governor of Oregon, made his fortune in the wool industry and his son, William, maintained a home in The Dalles and in Shaniko. William Moody managed the warehouses for his father. Life in remote Shaniko could be very comfortable. The Moodys would place telephone calls to The Dalles for fresh oysters from the Oregon coast that would be delivered by the railroad the next day. Fresh produce and meat was shipped along with ice for the ice boxes in the homes.

MAJOR EVENTS IN SHANIKO'S HISTORY

1872	Scherneckau settled at Cross Hollows
1879	Post Office established at Scherneckaus
1899	Shaniko Townsite Company formed
1900	172 living in Shaniko
1900	Construction Train reaches Shaniko
1900	1st Passenger train reaches Shaniko (6/1)
1901	Shaniko incorporates
1903	Shaniko becomes "Wool Capital of the World" $3 million wool sale, 1 million bushels of wheat shipped
1903	Severe smallpox epidemic
1904	$5 million wool sale
1910	Population reaches 600 according to US Census
1911	OR & NC completes railroad up Deschutes River Canyon
1911	Major fire destroys most of business area
1921	1st High School Graduation
1925	The Dalles-California Highway completed
1934	Last High School Graduation
1936	Last railroad passenger service
1942	Railroad freight service ends, tracks removed back to Kent
1955	Joe and Sue Morelli buy Shaniko Hotel
1964	Flood washes out remainder of Railroad
1978	Shaniko Hotel sold at auction
1980	Town receives National Historic District designation

MAP OF SHANIKO

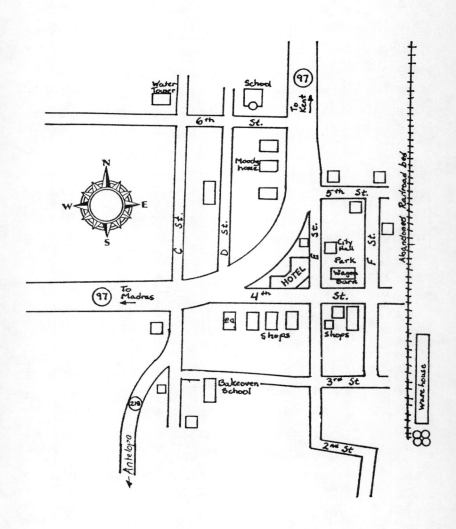

ANTELOPE

Antelope is located just eight miles from Shaniko on good paved roads on highway 218. A loop drive can be taken by following the highway west back to highway 97 and to the junction with the county road to Ashwood at Willowdale. From Willowdale, you can go north to the junction with highway 197 and return to The Dalles or stay on highway 97 and return to Shaniko, Kent, DeMoss and finally - Biggs Junction.

1897 CHURCH IN ANTELOPE

Only eight miles south of Shaniko lies the sleepy town of Antelope. From sleepy beginnings to the wild days of the west and of the Rajneesh takeover and back to sleepy origins, Antelope has seen its share of the wild west.

The Antelope Valley, from which the town gets its name, was named in 1862 by a group of supply freighters on their way to the gold fields of Eastern Oregon. This group included Joseph Sherar. Apparently, the valley was full of antelope, and hence the name. Antelope post office was established August 7, 1871 with Howard Maupin as the first post master.

Antelope was at the bottom of the long road grade up to Cross Hollows (and later, Shaniko). Serving as a stage stop on the road to Mitchell and John Day, the town had a slow beginning. When the Columbia Southern Railroad penetrated the area from Biggs to Shaniko, it became obvious that the line could never reach Antelope. Also, The Dalles-California Highway was constructed in 1925, and bypassed the little town.

Antelope had a wild side in the 1890's. It was a natural center for cattlemen, sheepherders and prospectors. Saloons and sporting houses serviced the lonely men. The little town had frequent shootings and brawls in the true western tradition.

A disastrous fire in 1898 started in Tom Condon's Bowling Alley (yes... Bowling alley ... cowboys needed something to do!). The fire spread quickly through the tinder dry business district of town and when the holocaust was over, only one building on main street remained. That building still stands at the far southern end of the main street.

The town quickly rebuilt, but would never regain its former glory. At about the same time, the upstart town of Shaniko was beginning to drain business and population away. The new town to the north eventually left Antelope an empty shell. Numerous other fires claimed more of the town. All that remains of the old town is the 1897 Methodist Church, a fraternal hall, John Silvertooth's Saloon, and a few scattered homes.

ANTELOPE SCHOOL - COMMUNITY HALL

In the 1980's, a new group of emigrants arrived. The Bhagwan Shree Rajneesh and his followers started their city of Rajneeshpuram on the site of the old Big Muddy Ranch. At first, they were just a curiosity in their red clothes. The Guru frequently drove through Antelope in one of his 42 Rolls Royces. But, the curiosity turned ugly when in 1984 the cult took over the town by a vote of 57 to 22 and renamed it Rajneesh.

The newcomers had little respect for the ranchers and residents of the area. Outnumbered, there was little the old-timers could do. The cult maintained a nude park in town. They renamed the only store and restaurant in town to "Zorba the Buddha", and generally made life miserable for everyone.

Followers of the Bhagwan and Antelope residents (and citizens all over the state) were sharply divided. Things came to a head when Ma Anand Sheela, spokesperson for the silent religious leader, left the country with a large amount of money. Within a short space of time, the Bhagwan was indicted on federal immigration fraud and deported to India after attempting to flee during a midnight escape.

The residents of Antelope voted to restore the original name to the town 32 to 0. Then they quickly voted to dis-incorporate their town to avoid any chance of a reoccurrence. The town has quickly reverted to a quiet town. Little remains to tell of the invasion of thousands of red-dressed cult followers of the Bhagwan. The Bhagwan even changed his name when he returned to India - Osho. (Osho died a few years after his return to India.)

MAP OF ANTELOPE

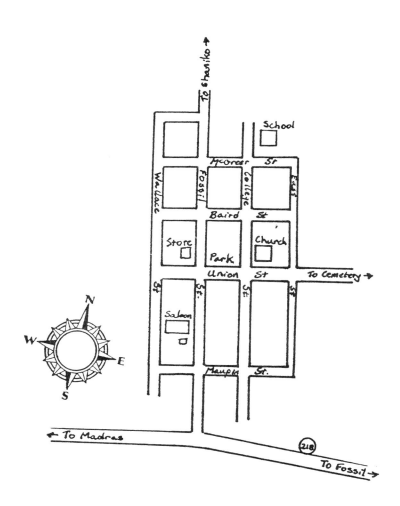

ASHWOOD

Ashwood is off the beaten path to say the least. It is 15 miles from Highway 97 and Willowdale. From Antelope follow the signs for Madras and Bend until the highway rejoins State Highway 97. Continue south a couple of miles to the turn off for Ashwood. The road is well maintained.

Along Trout Creek in Northern Jefferson County, lies the tiny town of Ashwood. The name applied was meant to note nearby Ash Butte and to commemorate Whitfield T. Wood, who settled in the area in the 1870's. The post office was established in 1898 and the first post master was James Wood, son of Whitfield Wood.

MAIN STREET OF ASHWOOD

Whitfield Wood came to the area to farm, but was soon disillusioned when the creek dried up in the summer and freezing nights began in August. Wood turned to raising cattle and soon the area was a well established cattle ranch.

In 1897, Thomas Brown, a sheepherder, found a gully of quartz near Trout Creek that had traces of silver and free gold. Quickly a boom town took shape on Trout Creek about three miles from the mining area and became Ashwood. The town was complete with saloons, hotels, livery stables, and stores.

The mines of Oregon King, Red Jacket, and Morning Star kept things going for a while. There were no smelters or milling facilities, so all of the ore had to be shipped out for processing. The mines didn't last long and the assay values kept dropping. It wasn't long until all of the mines shut down. Every so often, another strike would occur and revive interest in the area. In the 1920's, cinnabar was discovered at Horseheaven and Ashwood revived for a short time, but that boom ended soon, too.

People still inhabit the little valley. A modern one room school services grades k-4 on a slope overlooking the old main street. Old McCallum's Saloon was converted into a Baptist Church in the 1930's and the Ash Butte Grange still stands, one of the few false front buildings that survived the frequent fires that raged through the town. It is now a home.

MC CALLUM'S SALOON/BAPTIST CHURCH

KLONDIKE

Klondike can be reached from Highway 97 by travelling south from Biggs Junction to Wasco. Take the cutoff to Wasco and travel 2.4 miles into town. Turn left at Airport Road (signs indicate "Oregon Trail Auto Tour"). Go east 3.8 miles to the stop sign, turn right at the Oregon Trail tour route sign, and go 1/2 mile to Klondike. (Yes, the Oregon Trail went right through this area... but Klondike wasn't around then.)

KLONDIKE SCHOOL

Klondike never had a large population. In fact, the railroad crew that was building the Columbia Southern Railway south to Shaniko even deserted the town in the rush to reach the gold strike in Canada... hence the name

Klondike post office was established January, 11th, 1899 with A. B. Potter as the first post master. For a time, the name of the town was spelled "Klondyke" by the railroad. The post office lasted until November 30, 1951. Klondike had rail facilities, grain elevators (still standing), a store with livery stables, and an intriguing little brick school house. The school still stands, windowless, in the middle of a wheat field. The two story false-front store collapsed in on itself during the winter of 1993-94. The railroad tracks were removed following the abandonment of the rail line after the flood of 1964.

If you're heading south to Lonerock or Condon turn right on the gravel road just past the Klondike school, that will lead you back to Highway 206.

If you're going to Kent or Shaniko, retrace your path to Wasco and Highway 97.

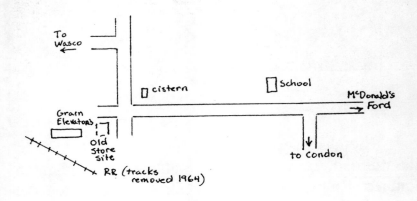

LONEROCK

Lonerock is located 21 miles east from Condon off Highway 206 to Heppner. The road is paved almost all the way to town with the exception of the last three miles. Once you get into Lonerock, though, the road is paved again.

Lonerock is an isolated community located on Lonerock Creek and was first established in 1875. The name is derived from the prominent rock that is located behind the Methodist Church. The rock itself stands 100 feet high and about 60 feet wide.

LONEROCK METHODIST CHURCH AND ROCK

Lonerock harkens back to an era when travel through the region was by horse and measured in days. Lonerock served as an outpost of civilization with its churches, stores and school. The town was founded by R.G. Robinson and Albert Henshaw in 1881 and was platted in 1882 as "Lone Rock", but the postal authorities switched the name to Lonerock.

This crossroads settlement still has its original jailhouse (1891) that was used extensively for the sheepherders who would stop in town to celebrate while on the way moving their flocks to higher pastures.

LONEROCK COMMUNITY HALL

An imposing school house was built in 1903 and still remains. It has lost its distinctive cupola and several attempts have been made to preserve it. The school closed its doors to students in 1961. The main street has a community center in an old false-front store. Several old houses line the neatly trimmed streets. Retirees maintain their yards and keep a sense of community alive. Residents have recently restored the 1898 church and adjacent parsonage.

LONEROCK SCHOOL

The automobile is probably to blame for the fate of most towns in North Central Oregon. Distances suddenly could be measured in hours rather than days. And busy little towns like Lonerock gave way to larger towns and markets.

A HOUSE IN LONEROCK

People began to move away from Lonerock after World War I. Water can be scarce at times and led to farming failures. The climate is rigorous, getting as low as 20 degrees below zero in the winter and 100 degrees above in the summer.

THE "ROCK"

The town has a population of about 25. The cemetery is located a few miles down the road past the church on a knoll overlooking the valley. It is well maintained and well worth the visit.

MAP OF LONEROCK

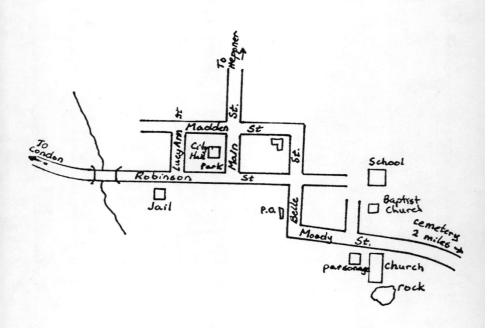

ELKHORN REGION OF EASTERN OREGON

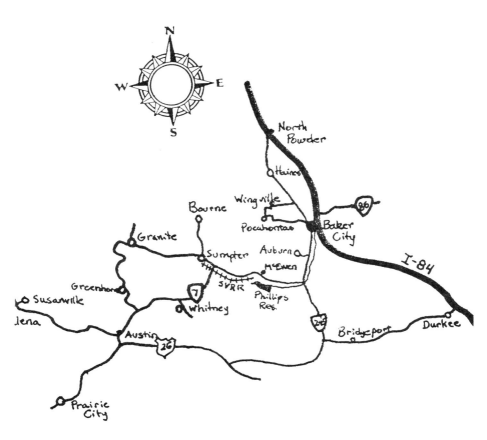

Baker County was established in 1862 just after gold had been discovered in the area in 1861. The region was quickly over run with goldseekers and the camp followers that came with them. Many towns had their beginnings around the mines but when the gold disappeared, so did the miners, and so did the inhabitants along with the town.

Gold was discovered in 1861 by Henry Griffen in Griffen Gulch just south of Baker City. Griffen and others had been searching for the legendary Blue Bucket Mine when he sunk a test hole and hit pay dirt. Towns like Auburn, Bourne, and Sumpter sprung into existence practically overnight. Auburn grew to be a tent city of 5,000 within one year. Inside of twenty years, many towns had already vanished, but Baker City rose to prominence and became known as the *Queen City of the Mines.*

Construction of the Sumpter Valley Railway in the late 1890's made the gold, timber, and livestock easier to bring to market and haul supplies and machinery back into the mountains. The railway owners were able to tap the vast wealth of the Elkhorn Mountain region.

The land that had been essentially empty of people except for the Native Americans that hunted or fished in the area, became infested with men searching for gold. In the rugged hills and canyons, wherever gold could be found, small mountain villages appeared with no thought of permanence. As time would show, some towns did last while others faded quickly into oblivion.

This is a look at the towns of the region that owe their existence to gold, the railroad, agriculture or forest industries of the region.

PEOPLE STILL SEARCH FOR THE MOTHER LODE

AUBURN

To get to the Auburn site travel west from Baker City on Highway 7 for 7.5 miles. Turn right onto Auburn Road and drive approximately 4 miles. The cemetery in located on the right side of the road over the hillside from an ancient apple tree grove.

Once one of the largest settlements in Eastern Oregon, Auburn now has no remains, other than what can be found in the lonely cemetery. After gold was discovered in the area in October of 1861, gold seekers flocked to the region and by June of 1862 Auburn was laid out by town founders Ed Cranston, George Hall, and William Packwood (grandfather of Senator Robert Packwood).

The main street ran from Freezeout Gulch to Blue Canyon, and building lots were taken on both sides. Within a short time, the mostly tent city had a population of 5,000. The post office opened in November of 1862 and operated continuously until October of 1903.

This rough and tumble mining camp was not a place for the tender hearted to mess with. Most of the time, vigilantes maintained what passed for law and order. Town council members passed laws that were nailed to the trees. Baker County was established in 1862, and naturally, Auburn, the only town, became the first county seat in September of that year.

The town had its share of saloons, dance halls, sporting houses, as well as, murders and lynchings.

The most famous murder and lynching was that of Spanish Tom in 1863. Spanish Tom had been gambling with Jack Desmond and Henri Larabee at one of the many saloons that Auburn had to offer. A quarrel ensued and the three went out into the street to settle their differences. Only Spanish Tom returned after he had stabbed the pair. He quickly left town, but was captured and returned to Auburn for justice. Tom was placed in a log cabin with guards watching over him.

A crowd of miners began to form and demanded that the trial take place on the hillside so that everyone could be present and hear the proceedings. Justice of the Peace Able allowed the trial to begin with Sheriff Hall and his men guarding Spanish Tom. At a signal the miners closed in and restrained the guards while another group dragged Spanish Tom toward the street. A rope was secured around his neck and dozens of men held on and ran through the street towards a nearby tree. Unfortunately, Tom's neck was broken long before they got him to a tree. The men strung him up and left him hanging as a warning to other shady gamblers.

Auburn aged as fast as it had grown. Gold in the immediate vicinity was getting harder to find and by 1864, the town was entering a speedy decline. In 1868, the new town of Baker City was elected to be the county seat and the records were removed from Auburn early one morning.

Auburn had gone from being one of the largest cities in Oregon to near extinction in less than 10 years. Spanish Tom is buried in "Boot Hill" along with Henry Griffen who started the whole gold rush with his discovery. All that remains of Auburn are these few tombstones four miles up a gravel road to nowhere.

MINE SHAFTS LIKE THIS
DOT THE HILLSIDES
NOT ALL OF THEM ARE COVERED OR
MARKED ... SO WATCH WHERE YOU WALK!

MC EWEN

  McEwen was named for Thomas McEwen, pioneer liveryman and stage operator. (The McEwen family eventually moved to the Burns and Nyssa area.) This small town was at one time the terminus for the Sumpter Valley Railway. Later, it served as a loading point for timber, livestock and some gold that was shipped to the smelter in Sumpter. McEwen had livery stables, a store, saloon, and railroad maintenance crew housing. Much of what was once the town was lost as the Sumpter Valley Dredge ate up the valley floor. All that remains is a store that serves the campers at Phillips Reservoir, a church and a few old houses. Nearby is the terminus for the current Sumpter Valley Railway. McEwen is located on Highway 7, 24 miles from Baker City.

SUMPTER

Sumpter is located 30 miles from Baker City just off Highway 7. The railroad operates on weekends. There is a park and museum at the Sumpter Valley Dredge.

Gold played an important part in the formative years of the town, fire nearly finished it off, and tourists keep it alive today.

Miners settled the area in 1862 and named the site after Fort Sumter in South Carolina. Post office records show that Joseph Young was the first post master in 1874, but at the time, Sumpter appeared on the Grant County rolls. This post office was closed in 1878, and reestablished in 1883 on the Baker County rolls. Mr. Young, once again, was the post master.

Some confusion still exists as to the variant spellings of Sumpter. Some say postal authorities wanted to differentiate between other Sumters, while some say it was named after a type of mule (sumpter mule). The town was platted in 1886. But, the town really didn't begin to blossom until after 1895.

Modern equipment used in gold mining helped make the mines more profitable and the coming of the railway to the region in 1896 provided the stimulus. From a population of 300 in 1897 to 4,000 in 1903, Sumpter became the center for the gold industry in Eastern Oregon.

The boom in hard rock mining brought a payroll that topped $2,000,000 in 1903. The narrow gauge railway delivered as many as six carloads of mining machinery per day and 600 carloads of timber a month were hauled to Sumpter or Baker City. In 1903, a smelter to process the ore was constructed in Sumpter and placed in operation. (The slag pile still remains, though the smelter is long gone.) At the peak of the boom in 1900, thirty-five mines in the region produced $9,000,000 of gold. (That is in 1900 dollars!)

ONE OF THE FEW REMAINING BUILDINGS THAT SURVIVED THE DISASTROUS FIRE OF 1917

During its peak, Sumpter boasted having a brick yard, sawmill, smelter, railroad, electric lights, reservoir and water system, and a main street made from wooden planks. There was a race track, baseball and basketball teams, undertaker, assayers, a brewery, dairy, two cigar factories, a China town, hospital, 16 saloons, a red light district, livery stables, five hotels, three general stores, a public school with 200 pupils, an opera house, two banks, four churches, a telephone system, newspapers and a fire department. Sumpter was certainly no back woods mining camp!

By 1906, the mines began to decline and close down. Towns in the area began to loose population and quiet down. Then, "Yuba" style dredge mining came to the valley in 1913 and things began to pick up again. The last of the mines closed in 1916, but two dredges were churning up the valley floor finding wealth in the sediment and gravel.

Disaster struck Sumpter on Sunday, August 13, 1917 that would deal a blow from which the town would never really recover. A fire began at the Capital Hotel and quickly spread throughout the business district of town. The fire department's hoses burned through and dynamite was used to blow up buildings to create firebreaks. By the end of the day, the prosperous town was reduced to rubble. Twelve city blocks were completely destroyed.

The structures that survived were the Odd Fellows Hall, the school, a few barns, one brick store, and most residences. The majority of the population moved on to greener pastures and those that stayed, scavenged the rubble to enhance their own homes.

ALL THAT'S LEFT OF THE BANK OF SUMPTER

Sumpter didn't die completely from the 1917 fire. The dredges kept working in the valley until 1924 before closing. The lull in gold mining activity lasted until 1935 when the massive dredge that sits in a lagoon beside Sumpter was built and began operation. It operated in the valley from 1935 to 1942 when it closed during World War II. (By law, all "non-essential" mining activity had to cease during the war.) Opening again in 1945, the dredge ran until 1954 when all dredging in the valley ceased.

SUMPTER VALLEY DREDGE
Measures 52 feet by 120 feet and weighs over 1250 tons. This equipment took over $4.5 million worth of gold from the valley floor.

This Dredge recovered more than $4.5 million in gold. The tailings from the three various dredges occupy the entire valley floor and thus eliminated a farming/ranching base for the community. Interestingly enough, the moonscape that was created by the dredging has become excellent habitat for a variety of water fowl and raptors.

The little narrow gauge railway that had made the tremendous exploitation of the region's wealth possible also faded into history in 1947. It was unable to compete with the expanding highways and the use of trucks. The railroad was dismantled and the equipment sold. Skagway, Alaska and places in South America, bought the running stock of the railroad.

A RIDE ON THE S.V.R.R.
Slow-paced fun from the past.

Later, a determined group of individuals restored several engines and rail cars and re-laid over seven miles of track. They operate the railroad as a tourist attraction and a functioning museum. It is well worth the time to ride in the train to get a sense of travel from the turn of the century.

Tourism now brings many people to Sumpter. New homes are scattered in among the old cabins. Motels and restaurants accommodate the hunters, would-be gold miners and antique bargain hunters that come to town on a regular basis. The population has been rising steadily since reaching a low of 100 in the early 1960's.

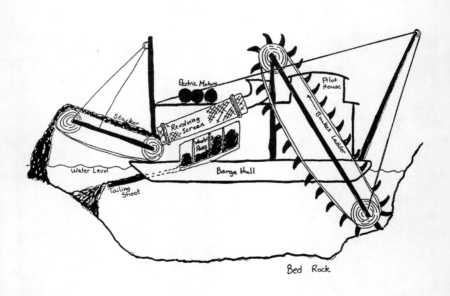

MAP OF SUMPTER

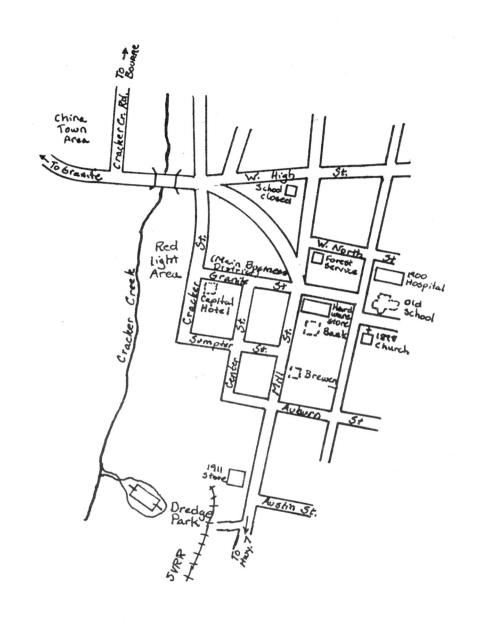

BOURNE

To get to Bourne, follow the road through Sumpter, cross over Cracker Creek and turn right on Bourne Road. Stay on the main gravel road for six miles until you reach town.

Bourne was named for Jonathan Bourne, Jr. of Portland, Oregon. He had an interest in several Eastern Oregon mines. He later went on to be a US Senator from Oregon (1907-1913). Bourne post office was established in March of 1895 and lasted until May of 1927.

Originally called "Cracker", Bourne was a mining and placering town in the 1870's. Located in a narrow canyon eight miles north of Sumpter, Cracker had only one street. The narrowness of the site didn't allow for much more. Occasionally, a short lane would hang on a cliff above the other buildings.

Cracker Creek provided enough water for placer mining in the early days, while later, hard rock mining techniques were used in the miles of tunnels that catacomb the hillsides.

ON THE WAY TO BOURNE
The Remains of a Dredge

At is peak, the town had a population of 1,500; two hotels, four saloons, seven general stores, two newspapers (one for locals, one for outside investors) three restaurants, two livery stables, and the obligatory red light district. One night the red light district suffered a fire, and while the crowds stood watching, the first man out of the burning building was the local preacher.

The Chinese were barred from the Cracker Creek region totally. The Chinese were despised by the local miners because of their hard-working natures and unfamiliar customs. Laws allowed whites to shoot Chinese if they were found in the upper valley of Cracker Creek.

ENTRANCE TO ONE OF MANY HARD ROCK MINES IN THE CRACKER CREEK REGION

The Columbia Mine produced over $3.5 million in gold in 1897 alone. But, the fortunes to be made in Bourne weren't always from legitimate mining. Of the two newspapers printed in the same shop; one was for legitimate news, while the other was meant for the outside world. Bourne entrepreneurs heralded vast gold deposits and sold shares in mines to people from all over the world. Myths that the town was only a thin skin over the mother lode were actively promoted. False claims brought in untold riches to unscrupulous speculators. When the mother lode never materialized, Bourne began a slow decline. Investors, wary of previous fraud, failed to provide the necessary investment to keep the hard rock mining operation functioning.

ONE OF MANY CABINS ALONG CRACKER CREEK

The post office closed in 1927 and the town began to revert to nature. In 1937, a cloudburst sent a wall of water down Cracker Creek that marked the real end of Bourne.

Remains of the town can still be found. Many cabins and foundations are found all along the old Main Street. Mining shafts and tailings can be seen on the hillsides above the road to Bourne. Some cabins are inhabited by gold seekers from a new era and some by those who are seeking a little mountain breeze and solitude.

"DOWNTOWN" BOURNE

GRANITE

Granite can be reached by driving through Sumpter and staying on the paved highway for 15 miles. The road climbs through some of the most scenic regions of Eastern Oregon.

Once a full-fledged ghost town with a population of one, Granite has seen a revival of sorts and now has a population of more than twenty. Though, if all the owners of property in town moved onto their land the population would probably exceed 500!

GRANITE CITY HALL

A.G. Tabor is credited with the discovery of gold on Granite Creek on July 4th, 1862. It wasn't long until miners were swarming all over the hills in the area. For a while the location was called Independence, to honor the date of the gold discovery, but with more than one Independence in the state, postal authorities balked.

A VIEW OF UPPER AND LOWER GRANITE

Granite City post office opened March 26, 1878 and didn't close until 1957 when the population had dropped to three.

The town was incorporated in 1899, with Grant Thornburg as mayor. Granite grew as new methods in hard rock mining made profits easier. The town had a grand 30 room hotel (which burned down in the 1940's), several smaller hotels, boarding houses, church, public school, city water system, telephone service, dance-hall, four saloons, jail, stores, red-light district, and a China town at the bottom of the hill.

In 1900, two gold nuggets worth $500 and $1800 were dug out from a spring in town. That same year, Tom Eagleton was murdered. Also, a tragic house fire almost cost several children their lives. Onlookers refused to go through the flames themselves to save the screaming children. "Madam Rose" from the "sporting house" saw the fire in time to run in and rescue the children, but in turn was severely burned herself. The heroic madam lingered for several days while no one would care for her burns. Finally, the local school marm took pity on the madam and dressed her wounds and tried to make her comfortable. She eventually died and the school marm was promptly run out of town for associating with a "loose-moraled woman".

As the gold mining era came to a close in the 1920's, several people hung on to Granite. Many families remained in the area eking out a living by working as loggers and doing part-time gold-mining.

MADAM ROSE'S HOUSE

MAIN STREET

With the re-valuation of gold in the 1930's many out of work transients arrived to live in the empty buildings attempting to strike it rich. Several of the town's major buildings were lost to careless fires during this era.

THE DANCE HALL

By 1956, only three men lived in the town full time. Ote Ford became the sole resident when the mayor hung himself, and "Cliff the Prospector" went looking for gold on Ten Cent Creek. Ote then assumed the jobs of mayor, town council, treasurer and constituency.

OTE FORD'S CABIN

Summer residents and fall hunters populate the town now. During the winter of 1996-7 there were 16 people who braved the cold and isolation A store located in "Old Granite" at the bottom of the hill has all the modern conveniences. Many of the old stores are still standing, though with every heavy winter snowfall, more roofs cave in. The 100+ year old school/city hall is a landmark behind the old Mercantile Building. Without some maintenance the Dance Hall may fall in at any time. Madam Rose's home is occupied and Ote Ford's cabin is still there...though Ote, himself, is now a resident of the cemetery.

GRANITE CEMETERY

The cemetery is full of historic tombstones and well worth the visit. It is located behind City Hall and can be reached by walking behind the A-Frame cabin that used to be "Sheriff" Bud Morrow's home. Tombstones can be found for the Thornburgs, Ote Ford, Madam Rose and Bud Morrow

BUD MORROW'S A-FRAME CABIN

A VIEW OF GRANITE

Bud Morrow was known as the "Sheriff of Granite" and kept the peace in the remote town during the 1960's through early 1980's. Bud's A-Frame cabin is near the cemetery where he is buried.

In 1982 Bud was murdered by Adeline Holleman who lived across the road from him. Adeline and her daughter Nora had waged a 10 year long running feud with Bud. He was shot while he sat in his rocking chair at his A-Frame cabin. Both women and an accomplice named Pasquale D'Onofrio landed in prison and mental institutions in the state. By 1995 all three had been released. Adeline still maintains her innocence. The investigation and trials cost Grant County over $180,000 making it the most expensive criminal case in the history of this small county.

With one or two new people moving to town every year, Granite is almost a "boom town" again. A stone marker at the bottom of the hill notes the discovery of gold. Buildings are marked with signs that tell of their original use. Be sure to respect the no trespassing signs and private property

MAP OF GRANITE

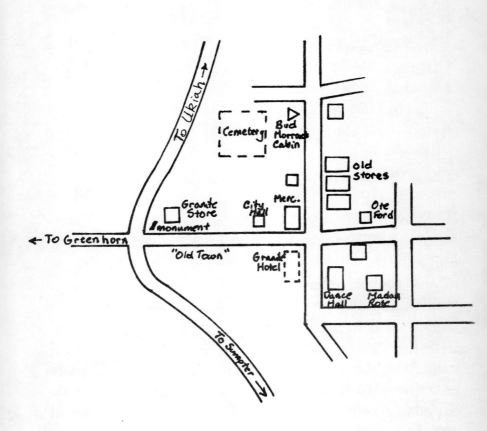

GREENHORN

Greenhorn can be reached from Granite by going straight across the highway on to a gravel road. Travel 1.3 miles and stay on the road designated for "Fremont Power House" (a great little side trip in itself!). Then, after 2.1 miles farther, turn left onto Road 13. Road 13 winds its way up the mountains over McWillis Gulch until it reaches the main road to Greenhorn. At the stop sign turn right and go 2.2 miles to Greenhorn.

The smallest and highest incorporated town in Oregon is how Greenhorn announces itself. At 6,200' elevation, it certainly is the highest! Mostly just summer cabins now, Greenhorn once boasted two hotels, two livery stables, city hall and jail, an assay office, local newspaper, two blacksmith shops and a red light district. With a population of 500 in the town and over 2,000 in the mining district around the hills, Greenhorn was a busy center of activity.

Named either for a prominent rock of green serpentine located on Vinegar Hill or for the inexperienced young men trying their hand at gold mining, Greenhorn began as a town in the early 1870's, but a post office was not established until May 24, 1902. The post office lasted until December 15, 1919. The town was incorporated in 1903 with E.G. Stevenson as mayor.

As the town grew, it exceeded its original fourteen acre limit. Voters approved a larger area and today the city limits extend to cover 53.58 acres. There were plenty of children in the town, but no school. At that time, the State of Oregon would not allow a school to be built near a saloon. So, with no permanent building, teacher Kate Mullen and the children were shuffled from one building to another, sometimes meeting in the Red Lion Hotel (which, by the way, had a saloon in the rear).

GREENHORN CITY HALL

Deep snows in the winter kept traffic to a minimum and people homebound for months at a time. Homes were austere and there was no electricity, but through the efforts of town-founder Simeon C. Richardson, water was piped directly to every kitchen in town. Sometimes the elk herds wallowed in the spring that provided the water, but that just gave the water more "body".

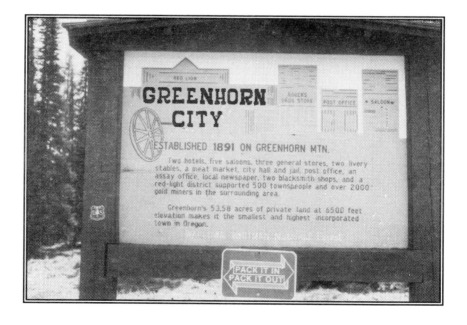

In 1912, Greenhorn became a genuinely unique town in the whole of the United States. A patent was issued to Richardson for the 53.58 acres in trust for the occupants of the town and their successors. By granting a direct patent to the municipality, the US government made Greenhorn a law unto itself, in effect a "principality". The patent was signed by President Taft and is currently owned by Baker County. The patent allowed the city to bypass the school laws that had caused the "mobile" school and allowed school to be held wherever the city fathers chose. (Which happened to be a vacant saloon.)

The Greenhorn mine operated until 1925. The increasing costs of mining and the lack of price increases for gold made the mines unprofitable to operate. Greenhorn was left to die a slow death.

SIGN IN "DOWNTOWN" GREENHORN

Fires took their toll on the remote town. One major fire began in the Red Lion Hotel and left most of Main Street in ashes. Square nails can still be found lying in the meadow that once was "downtown". Several old cabins remain. The old jail now resides in Canyon City. Summer homes dot the landscape and quiet solitude has taken over the once busy little town.

In the early 1970's, property owners in the city re-activated the city charter, which made the town legally incorporated again. There is an elected mayor and city council that fight to protect the land from developers and "progress". When cabins are built they must meet all building codes of the county and state. They must be plumbed for water and wired for electricity... even though electricity has never reached Greenhorn! The Oregon Blue Book gives the official Greenhorn population as three, while listing nine city officials.

While in "downtown" be sure to sign the guest registry located in the center of town by the flagpole. Remember to respect the no trespassing signs and be aware of the elevation...weather can change rapidly!

To return to Highway 7, retrace your route out of town and then stay on the main road downhill (11 miles).

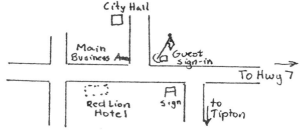

WHITNEY

A TOWN NAMED WHITNEY
RAILS OF THE SUMPTER VALLEY R. R.
REACHED WHITNEY VALLEY JUNE 1, 1901

ORIGINALLY A LUMBER COMPANY TOWN,
WHITNEY GREW TO BECOME THE MAIN
HEAD OF STAGE LINES TO MINING AND
CATTLE TOWNS SUCH AS UNITY,
BRIDGEPORT, AND MALHEUR CITY.

LOGGING RAILROADS WERE BUILT OUT OF
WHITNEY IN ALL DIRECTIONS DURING THE NEXT 20 YEARS.
NIBLEY LUMBER COMPANY SET UP A LARGE SAWMILL SOUTH OF
TOWN IN 1911 AS LOGGERS DAYLIGHTED THE GIANT STANDS OF
YELLOW PINE NEARBY. AT ONE TIME, OVER 150 PEOPLE CALLED
WHITNEY THEIR HOME WHEN THE RAILWAY WAS ABANDONED
IN 1947, THE TOWN CLOSED DOWN.

WALLOWA – WHITMAN National Forest

Whitney, located along Highway 7 between Sumpter and Austin was never a really a mining town in a region where mining was King. Though, some "doodle-bugs" (small dredges) did work the streams around Whitney with minimal success. The Sumpter Valley Railway reached the Whitney Valley on June 1st, 1901. The name for the little town came from the Valley, which was named for pioneer landowner, C.H. Whitney.

Almost exclusively a lumber company town, railroad spur lines were built in all directions funnelling the raw logs to the mill at Whitney. After the timber was cut into raw lumber, it was shipped on down the rail lines to Baker City. Nibley Company built a large saw mill at the south end of town in 1911. The mill burned in 1918 but, was rebuilt in

1938 by the Oregon Lumber Company. Five years later, the mill shut down when the timber supply was exhausted. The huge main building still stands, barely, on the edge of the old log pond. The surrounding mountains had heavy stands of Ponderosa Pine, Alpine White Fir and Yellow Pine. Using mostly clear-cut techniques, vast regions around Whitney were stripped of all trees in a relatively short period of time.

OREGON LUMBER COMPANY MILL
AT WHITNEY

The railroad was the life-blood of the town. It connected the remote location with Prairie City to the west and to Sumpter to the east. The second highest train trestle in the world at the time, spanned a gorge between Sumpter and Whitney. The impressive height made the trestle too shaky and it was removed in 1915 when the grade was run around the mountain instead. Centered between two terminals of the railroad, Whitney maintained a roundhouse and crew's quarters. Up to 14 rail crews were housed in Whitney at one time.

Except for hay, crops did not fare well at the high elevation. Cattle ranching kept many ranchers occupied supplying the beef to the crews at the railroad and the mines.

At least one attempt was made at large scale dredging for gold in the North Fork of the Burnt River Valley. In 1941 the Sunshine dredge was assembled just upstream from Whitney. It ran for about one year prior to being closed during World War II and for about one year after the war. It would appear that large scale dredging was not profitable in this area. The result is that the meadows remain for the cattle and deer to enjoy.

MAIN STREET

The winters in Whitney can be extremely severe. The temperatures dipped to 55 degrees below zero in the winter of 1919-1920. The school teacher at the time kept her pot-bellied stove red-hot but didn't feel warm until the temperature outside climbed back up to 50 degrees below zero. Frosts come early in August and last until late spring.

Many miners wintered in Whitney, but as soon as the thaw began on the hillsides, they were out prospecting again. Gold ore was shipped out on the railroad from nearby mines to the smelter in Sumpter.

The population never reached more than 200. It was always fluctuating, dependant on the mill and railroad workers. In 1910, the population had dropped to 55, and in 1950 it had reached zero.

With the closure of most mines and the end of the lumber mill, Whitney's fate was sealed. The railroad was removed in the 1940's. The tracks and even the roundhouse were taken away. Only a dozen houses and outbuildings remain on the dusty main street. The huge lumber mill stands south of town, a shadow of its former self. The cattle roam freely between the buildings and are the lone occupants of the little town in the beautiful little valley now.

If you want to return to the Baker City area just continue east on Highway 7 to complete a loop drive. Or, if you have lots of time, turn west and follow Highway 7 to Austin for a scenic drive to Galena and Susanville.

GALENA

Galena is located on Grant County Road #20 approximately 19 miles from the Junction on Highway 7 near Austin. Along the scenic route there will be a marker at Elk Creek noting the road to Susanville. (Four wheel drive is suggested if you take the two mile road up to Susanville.)

MAIN STREET

The townsite of Galena was once known as Susanville until about 1901 when the employees of a mine up Elk Creek decided they didn't like their mail being delivered so far away from where they worked and lived. They attained the post office and placed it at a point closer to the mine. Some stories claim that the miners stole the Post Office late one night - ink pad, canceling stamps and all, and took it back to the mining camp up Elk Creek. A new Post Office was petitioned for with the name of "Galena" to acknowledge that body of ore in the area. (Galena is a common lead, chemically known as lead sulphite.) The mining of galena seemed to be the best hope for the survival of the town, since most of the gold was played out by that time.

Galena's size never was very large, as most of the miners lived at their claims or in the mining company barracks near the mines. Though, 5000 men cast their votes at Galena in an worthless effort to have Galena designated the Grant County Seat. (Canyon City won the contest.)

Galena had a Chinese store, livery stable, hotel, dance hall, meat market and, of course, a number of saloons to entertain the miners during their free time.

For a few years, small "doodle bug" dredges worked the Middle Fork of the John Day River and creek beds getting the gold that earlier miners were not able to extract. At least one large dredge worked the Middle Fork. The Timms family built and operated a dredge below Galena in 1933. They dredged about 148 acres in six years time. The dredge was moved in

1939, but never saw operation again. Most all large ventures ceased operation when the gold began to run out. All gold mining operations ceased when "non-essential" mining was halted during World War II. Now only the "weekend" gold miners work the area still in search of the mother lode.

THE OLD GAS STATION

Without any base of commerce and very few travelers through the area, Galena began its long decline. The Post Office was finally closed in August of 1943 with papers going upstream to Susanville.

THE POST OFFICE

SUSANVILLE

Located a few miles up Elk Creek from its confluence with the Middle Fork of the John Day River was the old mining camp of Susanville. Originally it was referred to as "Upper Camp". The area had been established as a gold mining region as early as 1865 but did not get its "official" name until the miners absconded with the post office from the rival camp downstream. Gold was discovered in Elk Creek by John N. Reid. The camp that was located near the mouth of Elk Creek was named Susanville to honor Mrs. Susan Ward, one of the few women in the area and one of the earliest inhabitants.

REMAINS OF THE THREE-STAMP MILL IN SUSANVILLE

The Susanville Post Office was established on 12 September 1888, but was taken to the upper camp in 1901 while Galena post office was established near the original location. The Susanville post office was finally closed December 31, 1952 with papers being sent to the logging company town of Bates, 20 miles east.

The Armstrong nugget was discovered in the Susanville area in 1913 and is on display at the bank in Baker City.

Some of the mines that operated in the area were the Badger Mine, Bull of the Woods Mine, Gem Mine, Present Need Mine, and the Poor Man Mine. All of the mines paid well for a time.

UPPER END OF MAIN STREET

Susanville had only one narrow street, but at times there would be over 1000 miners in town for Saturday night festivities. A few cabins and the remains of a three-stamp mill at the upper end of town are about all that remind people that this area was once a hub of activity for many decades.

Return to County Road 20 and travel East back to Baker City, or West to the junction with Highway 395. (The road west is very scenic but slow going because of all the twists and turns as it follows the stream.)

WINGVILLE AND POCAHONTAS

A short loop drive out of Baker City takes you to two historic ghost towns of early Baker County. Take old Highway 30 north from Baker City about three miles to "Wingville Road". Turn left onto Wingville Road and go west about two miles.

WINGVILLE is noted for its very historic cemetery. Settled by Southern Democrats loyal to the Southern Cause and many of them ex-soldiers in Price's Army, the area was known as the "left wing of Price's Army" and after that, "Wingville." A post office was established in 1871 and discontinued in 1879. The cemetery is full of excellent tombstone art and poetry. An interpretive sign is located in the yard of the "Mayor of Wingville". The large building there is the combined structures of an I.O.O.F. hall and a church. These two structures were dragged together and combined to make the grange hall.

Continue straight west for 1 1/2 miles and turn left, another 1/3 mile to a right hand turn and a short distance will bring you to the cemetery.

Go west another 1/2 mile and turn left. Go South for about one mile to the site of Pocahontas.

Located northwest of Baker City is the ghost town of POCAHONTAS. A town had been laid out along Pine creek a few miles southwest from the

Pocahontas site and was originally called Pine City. The Pine City residents were persuaded to move to the Pocahontas site within a short time after Pine City was born. The Chandler Wagon Train of 1862 settled the area at the base of the Elkhorn Mountains as a farming community. The Chandler cabin is currently located in "Downtown" Haines.

Pocahontas had a hotel, express office and blacksmith shop. Travelers through the Baker Valley, in early years, had to travel close to the base of the mountains to avoid the marshy valley floor. A post office was established in August 4, 1863. Pocahontas' main claim to fame is that it received 10 votes when the state legislature was trying to decide where to place the state capitol. Inconclusive records report that the Pocahontas Post Office closed either in June of 1864 or in 1872.

To return to Baker City, follow the signs from Pocahontas (approximately seven miles).

NORTH AND SOUTH OF THE WALLOWAS

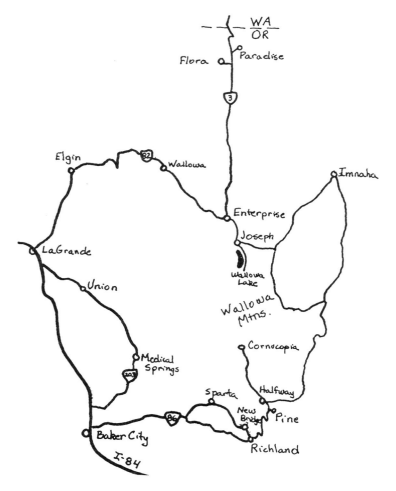

SOUTH OF THE WALLOWAS

SPARTA

Sparta is a ghost town located on the southern edge of the Wallowa Mountains. It is easy to get to and, along with Pine and Cornucopia, makes a very nice day trip out of Baker City. From I-84 take Exit 302 and travel east past the Oregon Trail Interpretive Center. About 21 miles east of the freeway will be a left hand turn onto a gravel road marked "Sparta 9 miles". This gravel ride ascends out of the Powder River canyon to reach the plateau above. After a few miles of turns and great vistas the road passes a fine old stone house on the left. Just stay on the main route until you reach the stone store at Sparta.

Sparta is yet another town founded by William H. Packwood (Auburn was his the first. William H. is an ancestor of US Senator Robert Packwood). Sparta was named by Packwood for his hometown of Sparta, Illinois.

Packwood had come to the Sparta region in 1871 along with I.B. Brown, Ed Cranston and C.M. Foster from Baker City to prepare for the building of a ditch (the Sparta Ditch). They laid out a townsite and decided to spin a four-sided top with a proposed name for the town on each side. Packwood's selection won the spin.

SPARTA STORE

The Sparta post office was established October 29, 1871 with Lynn White as the first postmaster. A nearby mine named the "Gem" mine may have had an earlier post office that converted to the Sparta name and moved a short distance to the new townsite.

The Gem along with the gold strikes in Shanghai Gulch and Maiden Gulch demanded a large quantity of water to operate the placering gear.

Packwood backed the Sparta Ditch venture that brought water from 32 miles away to the placer mines. But, by then the gold was beginning to run out.

Chinese workers moved into the area to re-work the tailings. Chinese workers were used to dig the Sparta Ditch - a feat accomplished in less that two years. (Compare that with any public works project of today - its hard enough to go 32 feet let alone 32 miles in two years!)

Both facts and legends surround the treatment of the Chinese during the gold mining era. Certainly, many atrocities did occur. One legend is that of the Lily White mine located north of Sparta. Allegedly, 13 Chinese miners (some claim as many as 100) were buried alive inside the mine when the entrance was dynamited shut to avoid paying the miners' wages when the gold ran out. No hard facts remain to support this legend. Locals claim though, that on moonlit nights, the Chinese miners reappear to sing and dance near the mine entrance.

By 1915 all the hard rock mining had ceased and then around 1917 the placer mines quit working the land. The ditch lived on though for many years to be used by the cattlemen and farmers in the area.

TOWN GULCH HOUSE

The only buildings that remain are the Sparta Store, a heap that remains from a collapsed building and three homes, as well as the cemetery. (The cemetery is located on "Boothill" across Town Gulch from the store. It is on private property - please do not trespass.) The collapsed building was the Town Gulch House, an early boarding house in Sparta. It was built around 1868 and lasted until a heavy snowfall took it down in 1989. Chinatown was located along Town Gulch near where a pond is currently located. Down the road near a dilapidated chicken house was the Sparta School site.

The stone store was built in 1872 by W.H. Heilner. The store operated until 1930 and is located on the original Main Street of Sparta. It is 24' by 50' and is made of quarried tuff. The walls are 30" thick. Tuff is volcanic in nature, easy to cut and then hardens when exposed to the elements.

ON THE WAY TO SPARTA

The last post office for Sparta was located in a house about 200 feet west and on the other side of the road from the stone store. Mable Binns was Sparta's last postmaster when it closed October 1, 1952.

If you keep traveling easterly on the main road in Sparta you will descend into New Bridge in about 9 miles. New Bridge was originally on the banks of Eagle Creek near where a pioneer bridge was built across that stream. The New Bridge Post Office was established in 1878 and closed in 1967. Originally in Union County, New Bridge was part of a long panhandle that in 1901 was ceded to Baker County. Once back on the pavement, follow the signs to Richland and then the main road to Halfway. Just before coming into Halfway a sign notes that Pine is one mile from the Highway. Turn right onto the Pine access road. There is a small interpretive wayside stop that has some great panels describing the history of the region.

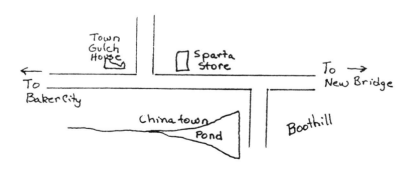

PINE

Pine post office was established in June of 1878 with the name Pine Valley. Originally part of Union County (until the panhandle was ceded to Baker County) Pine Valley never became a large town. In 1879 the post office was located at the Greener farm which was approximately two and one half miles from the present site of Pine. The name Pine Valley was shortened to just Pine in 1892. All that remains of Pine are a stone store and a few assorted buildings.

The Pine Valley was first settled in 1862 when the Tim Goodell wagon train reached the valley and decided to settle. The town of Pine was on the original route over the mountain from Eagle Valley. Early stage and motor car travel played an important role in maintaining a "business district" of sorts at Pine. With a store and gas station, Pine served travelers, truckers and miners headed up into the mountains. Later, the newer highway system bypassed Pine and its importance as a gas station stop quickly faded.

ACROSS FROM THE STORE

CORNUCOPIA

Go on into Halfway and explore there for a bit, then head up the road into the mountains to Cornucopia. Be aware that the last six miles is a single lane gravel road and climbs rapidly from the valley floor. Cornucopia is at the end of the road about 12 miles from Halfway. The road will take you through "Jim Town" and Carson. Both of these sites once vied for prominence in Pine Valley and lost out to Halfway.

Gold was discovered in the Cornucopia district in 1870. Between 1880 and 1941 over 315,000 ounces of gold was taken from the area. (Multiply that number by the current gold prices and you'll get an idea of how rich the gold deposits were!) Gold, silver and copper were all mined in this region. Most of the ore was shipped to the smelter in Tacoma, Washington via the railroad depot at Robinette.

Cornucopia is Latin for "Horn of Plenty" and is an apt title for the area. A post office was established in the mining camp on December 7, 1885 and ran until June of 1942 when the mines were closed during World War II. and President Roosevelt closed all unnecessary mining to save dynamite and powder for other uses.

Some of the longest mine shafts in the United States are located in the hills around here. It is estimated that there are 6,300 feet of shafts and 36 miles of underground tunnels. Recent gold mining activities has brought the region back into the news because of environmental concerns. Cyanide was used to leach the ore and can still be found in the area.

ENTERING CORNUCOPIA

Mountains almost encircle the Cornucopia townsite. Cornucopia Mountain, Granite Mountain, Red Mountain, Mt. Roosevelt, Mt. Way Up and Simmons Mountain. There may have been 66 mining claims that worked 27 ledges at the beginning of Cornucopia's mining industry. All of those claims were within four miles of the townsite.

The townsite is at 4,700' elevation and due to its close proximity to steep mountain slopes sometimes has recorded snows of 15' depth in the streets of town. Often time avalanches came roaring down the slopes and destroyed mining buildings and even homes. As late as 1923 an avalanche came down the hillside and killed three members of the Fisher family as they sat in their mining company house.

MINING COMPANY BUNKHOUSE

Cornucopia experienced several big booms during its life. The first boom occurred from 1884 through 1886. The town was then located a mile or more downstream from its current location. The early town had five saloons, one store, two restaurants, and a blacksmith shop when the post office was first established.

The town's growth naturally migrated north towards the mines and mill structures. Eventually the main part of town was almost a mile further upstream from its original location.

MAIN STREET LOOKING SOUTH

By 1898, the 20 acres of platted town included two stores, several boarding houses, an hotel, two restaurants, two taverns, dance hall, jail, blacksmith shop with livery stable, post office and a school. Electricity was available - the first electricity in the Panhandle region. The mines and town were on separate electric power plants.

At the turn of the century the major mines were: The Last Chance Mine, The Mayflower Mine, Queen of the West Mine, The Red Jacket Mine, The Simmons Mine, The Union-Companion Mines, The Way Up Mine, The Whitman Mine, and The Wild Irishman Mine. The last company to operate gold mining prior to World War II was the Cornucopia Gold Mines Company which took over in 1930 and brought several of the mines into their biggest production under a single operator. The company ceased to exist in 1941. Records show that three mines - The Red Jacket, The Last Chance, and The Union-Companion mines produced the bulk of the gold, silver and copper. Nearly 700,000 pounds of copper were taken from the Last Chance mine between 1933 and 1941. The mine employed up to 100 men, working three shifts as late as 1939.

A short-lived town was located about one mile south of Cornucopia in 1885. Allentown grew up around the Allen family cabin. It had several business and a mill, but they all quickly threw their lot in with Cornucopia when that town began to boom.

Several major buildings have been lost to heavy snowfalls in Cornucopia over the past ten years. The post office and drug stores, both often photographed landmarks, have both tumbled down. A bunkhouse, several cabins and lumber piles are all that are left to remind us of the hard working people that once braved the harsh winters and the difficult labor in the tunnels.

THE REMAINS OF THE POST OFFICE

NORTH OF THE WALLOWAS

FLORA

Located 32 miles north of Enterprise on the breaks of the Grand Canyon of the Grande Ronde River is this agricultural community ghost town. The only way practical way to get from the south side of the Wallowa Mountains to the north side is to go around them. There is a road that goes from the Halfway area to the Imnaha region or on to Joseph - but check for local road conditions at the forest service before attempting this trek. Flooding is 1997 washed a lot of that road out and re-construction may take several years. The other alternative is to return to I-84 and head north to La Grande and take state Highway 82 to Enterprise. Take State Highway 3 north out of Enterprise to get to Flora.

Flora was named for Flora Buzzard, the daughter of the first Post Master; Adolphus D. Buzzard. The Post Office opened October 6, 1890 and closed Dec. 27, 1966. Flora Buzzard Cobb lived to be 107 and died in 1991.

The Flora townsite was originally called Johnson Meadow for homesteader Frank Johnson, the town was plated and surveyed on his farm. A school was begun for the children of all the homesteaders in the area as early as 1891. The first school stood at the intersection of four section lines to avoid valuable land from being used. This corner became known as Buzzard's Corner for the Buzzard family that lived nearby.

THE FLORA SCHOOL

A general merchandise store opened in 1895 near the school house and soon after, three blacksmith shops, a general store, a hotel, churches and the Flora Lumber Company were operating in the new town. The first store was operated by A.P.Davis.

A fire in 1896 destroyed the 1895 store, but it was rebuilt almost immediately. Flora was platted in 1896 by Frank S. Johnson, the local blacksmith. A general store was opened by W.H. Baker in 1897 and about the same time the Flora Lumber Company was also organized.

The Methodist Episcopal Church was erected in 1898 and a Christian Church was in operation by 1902. The Flora Hotel opened in 1898 as well. Other stores at the turn of the century included a photographers studio, a millinery and dressmaking shop, a lumber yard, a sawmill and two shingle mills. Also, Flora had its own newspaper - the *Flora Journal* beginning in 1899.

THE FLORA METHODIST CHURCH

Flora continued to grow steadily and by 1908 was experiencing a seemingly ever expanding construction and agricultural boom. The Flora State Bank was doing a good business. Also, Flora received a Flour Mill in 1908. It should be noted that there has been no mention of a tavern or saloon - that's because Flora never did have any!

In 1915 the "new" school was constructed two blocks north of the main business district on a slight rise. The school is two stories high with a bell tower. Flora had a very modern school for its location and time - and it was the only high school available in the north part of Wallowa County. In 1926 Flora School had the largest graduating class ever - fifteen. The graduating class of 1940 had five. The high school continued until 1962 when a bus system started transporting the 12 freshman, sophomores, juniors and seniors to attend high school to Enterprise. Finally, the elementary school consolidated with Enterprise and began busing the younger students in 1977. All the school equipment was sold at auction - including the school bell. It sold for $680 on the condition that it remained in the bell tower.

The closing of the post office in 1966 and the school in 1977 really sealed the fate of the town of Flora.

Flora's glory days were the years between 1890 to just after World War I. It was the center of commerce and social life for the entire region. Travel to Flora was either through Enterprise to the south or Anatone, Washington to the north. The main crop of the area was wheat. But, being so far from the markets, many farmers raised the wheat and then fed it to hogs, which they then herded to market in Anatone or Enterprise. Decreasing population due to consolidation of tiny homesteads into more economically feasible sized ranches, mechanization of farming practices, a downturn in the timber industry, poor transportation and proximity to markets helped cause the demise of Flora. Farming is always risky considering the climate around Flora. The population had to adjust to the ability of the land to support people.

Currently, Flora still has the lovely old school (attempts are being made to restore it and list it on the National Register of Historic Places), the M.E. Church, the old Flora State Bank building (its the building that has stairs going up the outside to the second floor that and has been converted to a residence), a store front, a few old houses and a great cemetery. (The cemetery is an interesting place to wander around.)

MAP OF FLORA

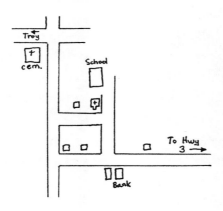

PARADISE

The road to Paradise is near the junction of the Flora cutoff on Highway 3. Take the second turnoff on the right marked Paradise. Continue east for a couple miles to get to the Community Hall. Less than a mile further is the Deer Creek School Building. It is a well maintained gravel road. The Paradise Cemetery is located about a mile and a half north of town

The only building left in Paradise is the Paradise Community Hall, which was built in 1912 as a church.

In 1878, three men named Wade, Holley and Masterson moved their cattle into the Paradise area thinking it would be an excellent location to winter cattle. Tragically, it was a particularly bad winter and most of their cattle were killed. They left the following spring, but the name Paradise stuck to the region.

A few years later, George Allen built a cabin in the area and became a permanent resident. He was followed by Lincoln Austin in 1884. A store opened in Paradise in 1885, followed by a blacksmith shop in 1890. Eventually, the town grew to include a post office, log hotel, a store, livery stable, a sawmill and several other buildings.

Around 1935, the community got together and repaired the abandoned church to create the Community Hall. They removed the steeple and bell, propped up the foundation and gave it a coat of paint.

The building has since been used for various social functions and by social clubs.

The Paradise school was located about three miles from town. Actually, the Deer Creek school was closer to town. A new school replaced the old building in the early 1950's. Deer Creek School operated until 1962 when it consolidated with Enterprise and the few remaining children in the area were bused there. (This was a major blow to the Flora School District. Had Deer Creek school and nearby Promise school merged with Flora, the consolidated school would have been more economically feasible to maintain. As it turned out, Flora School lasted only a few years longer.)

The Deer Creek School was "revived" of sorts in the early 1980's. Several ranchers in the area balked at sending their young children on the long bus rides daily to Enterprise. The Dave Jackman and Don Franklin Families opted to repair the old school, hire a teacher and operate a private school for six children. Another family sent over their kindergartner to join the school. The teacher lived in a 30' travel trailer parked next to the schoolhouse. In 1983 and 1984, Mr. Jackman taught the private school himself. But the school closed when the Jackman family moved into Enterprise in 1985.

The Paradise school was located a few miles to the north and operated until 1963 when it too, merged with Enterprise. Unfortunately, the school building burned to the ground in 1991.

An early road down to Ray's/Hansen's Ferry which crossed the Grande Ronde River, was through Paradise and down Deer Creek. In 1947, when Highway 3 was completed, this older route was abandoned, and what remained of Paradise was left in the middle of nowhere - just where Paradise is usually found.

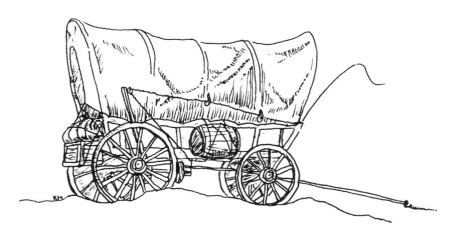

OTHER GHOST TOWNS IN EASTERN OREGON

ALBEE

Albee is located in southern Umatilla County near Ukiah six miles off Highway 395. The turn off is located on Highway 395 between Ukiah and Battle Mountain. The well maintained road is clearly marked.

Near Albee at a turn in the road, there are several stone monuments commemorating several events in the history of the area.

One states:
"The Tears or Sorrow
Grief & Sacrifice
Connell
1878-1889
Gracie
Pearlia
Gertie
Mark
Cleo
Baby
On This Meadow
All Are Flowers
Tom Gilliam 1863
Dollie Gibson 1878"

And on the reverse states:

"Pioneer History
1860, 1890
Two Stone Sites
Lot 2 NW 1/4 Sec 19
Granted by Pete French
Dec. 11 1990
July 24 1992
Drovers Herders
Indians Teamsters
Ranchers Settlers
Miners Soldiers
Hunters Trappers
At this place all trails
Crossed"

Another marker is inscribed:

"Battle of Camas Prairie
1 mile SW 4 July 1878

2000 Warriors	33 Volunteers
Cayuse Bannock	Under
Paiute Tribes of	J. Wilson
Grey Eagle son of	Wm. Ellis
Buffalo Horn	J. Delivan
Egan	B. Beagle
Oytes	J. Connell
Umapine	H. Connell

Tendoy   A. Knight
                                W. Homar

3 Log Forts Built
1879-81 Ft. Snipe 1881
Killed by ???
Ft. Wilson NW
Ft. Camas
5 miles S."

MARKER NEAR ALBEE

A mile of more south of the markers is the townsite of Albee. A post office was located in this area 17 June 1881 and was originally named "Snipe". (Probably for nearby Snipe Creek or for "Ft. Snipe").In 1882 the name was changed to "Alba". The town was platted in 1887 with the name *Alba*. Sometime around the turn of the century the name of the town was changed to *Albee* for the Albee brothers, well-known local stockmen. The Post Office officially made the change to Albee in July of 1907.

DOWNTOWN ALBEE

The town was mostly a stage station, stockman's supplier and community center for the ranchers of the area. At its peak prior to World War I, Albee boasted a hotel, stage office, two stores, blacksmith shop, school, church and "Dick's Dance Hall". Almost all of the buildings were located along the main stretch of road. The "upstart" town of Ukiah a few miles south lured away the businesses since it was better situated at the crossroads of the new state highways. Albee struggled through the ravages of the depression in the 1930's but World War II drained away the people in search of better jobs. The nature of ranching changed and fewer hands were needed to operate the stock ranches which had mostly converted to cattle ranches. The post office closed on October 31st, 1943.

ALBEE SCHOOL

Several old buildings remain, though all are on private property. (Please respect the no trespassing signs.) The schoolhouse is still standing. It was built in 1928 to replace a larger school that had burned down the year before. The school was in operation until the mid-1940's when the few remaining students were then bused to Ukiah. The other building were victims of fire and scavengers in search of lumber to mend barns and other out buildings.

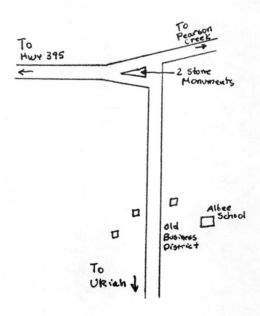

BAKEOVEN

Located on the highway that connects Shaniko and Maupin is the old community of Bakeoven. A teamster with a load of flour destined for the gold fields of John Day was stranded in the area when Native Americans ran off his mules. Not despairing, the enterprising man constructed an oven from rough clay and stones and made bread to sell to the prospectors on their way to the mines. A post office was established in 1875 and discontinued in 1913, with mail going to Flanagan. Flanagan was in turn discontinued with the post office re-established at Bakeoven in 1914. The small community has lost its old school house which now resides in Shaniko. All that remains are a farmhouse and a few outbuildings. A large barn has "Bakeoven" painted on its front. Don't blink or drive too fast or you'll miss the entire "town".

DEMOSS

DeMoss is located on Highway 97 between Wasco and Moro. This was little station on the railroad. The post office was called DeMoss Springs. The station was named for the famous pioneer family of the area that had toured Europe and North America under the name of the "Lyric Bards". The patriarch of the family was Professor James M. DeMoss (who had been the founder of the town of North Powder). A county park is all that is at the site now.

DURKEE

Located about 20 miles south of Baker City and just off I-84 is the community of Durkee. The area was well known to Oregon Trail pioneers as the Express Ranch. C.W. Durkee was the first postmaster in 1865. The town was later the site of a Wells Fargo stage station. For a time the post office was moved to Weatherby, but was returned to Durkee. The name *Durkee* was officially used beginning in 1902 in honor of the first settler. The railroad came to Durkee in 1883. An interesting old stone schoolhouse remains along with a few old storefronts.

HARDMAN

Located 21 miles south of Heppner on State Highway 207 is the ghost town of Hardman. In the 1870's two towns a mile apart vied for the business of the freight wagon drivers and stagecoach riders. Raw Dog and Yallerdog fought over the passengers, even bribing the drivers to change hotels after they had settled in for the night.

A post office was located in Raw Dog when it was determined that more people lived there than in Yallerdog. Shortly thereafter, the residents of Yallerdog gave up the fight and moved into Raw Dog. Postal Authorities balked at the idea of a town named

Raw Dog, Dog Town or even Dairyville, so the name of the first settler in the area was applied to the new town. Mr. Hardman just happened to also be the first post master. The post office operated with intermissions from 1882 until its final closing in 1968. With the disappearance of stagecoaches the purpose for the town began to fade away. Even the gas station was hardly needed anymore.

Several old store fronts remain and a few old homes. All are on private property. Hardman also has an interesting cemetery on the hill above town.

MEDICAL SPRINGS

Located 22 miles north of Baker City on Highway 203 was a world famous health resort, complete with a full medical staff. Native Americans had used the hot sulphur spring waters for healing for centuries prior to the arrival of the settlers.

NARROWS

Narrows is located about 25 miles south of Burns on State Highway 205. There are also several other would-be towns/ghost towns in the region such as Lawen, Diamond, Brothers, Wagontire, Happy Valley, Frenchglen, Andrews, Danner, and more. Most of them are remote so check with locals for current road conditions.

The Narrows is what locals describe this piece of land located between Harney and Malheur lakes. Situated on the Burns-Frenchglen Highway, the town recieved a post office in 1892 and with an intermission closed permanently in 1936. In the 1980's after several wet years, the water level of the two lakes had risen enough to require that the highway level needed to be raised as well. By that time there was little left of the old community. Anything that was left was soon under water. With no natural outlet these bodies of water ill continue to fluctuate.

Narrows was established by Charles Haines as a center for his ranching interests but it became an important way station for travelers to far reaching ranches. Soon the ranch house was joined by a hotel, several saloons, a store, a livery stable and a gambling hall. A solid stone jail was constructed and a handsome frame schoolhouse as well. Both were located side by side - perhaps as a deterrent to the rowdies in the classroom or an incentive to improve oneself for those in the stone jail.

As roads were improved and more ranchers got trucks and cars, The Narrows had little to offer them in comparison to the big shopping metropolis of Burns. Ranchers instead drove into the "Big" city and left little Narrows to die a slow death. Now, no one lives in Narrows and there is little to remind you that there was once a town at this site. Vandals and treasure seekers had almost carted away the whole town by 1966, the rest had to be razed to prevent fires.

OLEX

In northern Gilliam County on Highway 19 is this misnamed ghost town. The town is about 15 miles south of I-84 and Arlington. The name was intended to be Alex, but the petitioner had such poor handwriting, the officials in Washington thought he meant Olex, and that is what it has always been since the post office was established in 1874. A great two story turn of the century store with a second story dance hall, and an old flour mill is about all that remains in Olex region.

RICHMOND

Located in Wheeler County on Highway 207, north of Mitchell, this small town was named for the confederate capital by a friend of the founder for the prime mover in the community, who was also had "rebellious" tendencies. An excellent old church and several old store fronts still remain.

Early Mack

Thorny Fence

Sunderland's Kink

WHERE HAVE ALL THE PEOPLE GONE?

Why did Eastern Oregon "de-populate"? Many of the towns that have been discussed had very large populations at one time. Sumpter had 4,000. Auburn had 5,000. Where did they all go?

Many reasons come to mind. In the case of the gold mining towns many of the inhabitants were single men out seeking their fortune. When word of gold strikes elsewhere came, they went. (Such as the case of the railroad crews who abandoned work at Klondike so they could go to the Yukon.) Gold was being found and mined all over the west in the late 1800's and a transient population tended to follow the strikes.

Some of the towns depopulated because of market crashes, such as Shaniko. The demand for wool was greatest in the United States just prior to and including World War I, but after that, wool growers in Australia and other parts of the world could provide the shrinking market with less expensive raw materials. Sheepherders all over the west got out of the wool business.

In the wheat growing regions, mechanization led to a decrease in labor demands. In the early 1880's wheat harvest was very labor intensive, requiring large numbers of men to handle to mules, move the grain, and sew the sacks. In time, the need for such large crews decreased, even though more land went into production. Today, three or four people can do the work of 30 workers in less time. Small towns that held the families of the men that worked the large ranches, and the blacksmith, harness makers and livestock ranchers were no longer needed.

The lumber industry has undergone a long decline in the past forty years. Early logging practices in Eastern Oregon tended to wipe out extensive stands of marketable timber. Lumber mills all over the region began to close or consolidate into larger towns as supplies diminished and competition between companies drove some from the market. The vast timber resources around Whitney were almost wiped out by the 1940's. Only now, with managed care, are the forests re-appearing. There is marketable timber, but again, modern techniques have reduced the need for such a large labor force as was required in the past.

With the advent of the automobile and the trucking industry, along with the highway system, larger towns and better markets were available to the rural farmers. Consequently, small towns went into decline when they could no longer compete.

Many homesteaders had settled in the area and utilized the small towns for their services, schools and churches. Unfortunately, as the farm scene changed from less labor intensive to higher mechanization, the small farmer had a more difficult time making a profit. Much of the land was marginal to begin with. 160 acres could not support a family. So, ranches became larger and larger and the small farmers sold out or consolidated. With fewer people around, the small service centers had an ever shrinking market to supply, until they too were forced out.

Eastern Oregon didn't depopulated overnight. It was a long process that can still be seen happening in some areas. The big influx of people in the era of 1862 through 1900 had to adjust as the potential of the land as resources became more apparent.

HOMESTEAD ACT OF 1862

The U.S. Congress passed the Homestead Act which made is possible for a person to obtain 160 acres of land for the following qualifications:
>Must be head of the household or
>21 years old
>A citizen of the U.S. or
>filed a declaration of intent to become a citizen
After getting the 160 acres the claimant needed to:
>Pay a filing fee
>Live on the property
>Make certain improvements
At the end of the five years a clear title was given to the homesteader. By 1900 over 600,000 farmers had clear title to their lands. The Homestead Act was modified many times over the years before it was finally repealed in 1977.

As the Homestead Act was used to settle Eastern Oregon, it became very apparent that, in most cases, 160 acres was not enough land for a farmer or rancher to make a living.

GOOD THINGS TO READ AND RESEARCH

A PICTORIAL HISTORY OF GILLIAM COUNTY, OREGON Gilliam County Historical Society (c) 1983 Taylor Publishing Co. Portland, OR 176 pages

A PLACE CALLED ANTELOPE: THE RAJNEESH STORY Donna Quick (c) 1995 August Press, Ryderwood, WA ISBN 0-9643118-0-1 152 pages

ANTELOPE The Saga of a Western Town Art Campbell (c) 1990 Maverick Publications, Bend, OR ISBN 0-89288-132-1 326 pages

BAKER COUNTY SKETCH BOOK Gordon and Patricia Stewart (c) 1956 40 pages

DICTIONARY OF OREGON HISTORY Edited by Howard McKinley Corning (c) 1989 Binford & Mort Publishing, Portland, OR ISBN 0-8323-0449-2 281 pages

EARLY OREGON ATLAS Ralph N. Preston (c) 1978 Binford & Mort Publishing, Portland, OR ISBN 0-8323-0304-6 60 pages

FROM THE WALLOWAS Grace Bartlett (c) 1992 Pika Press, Enterprise, OR ISBN 0-918957-08-7 142 pages

GHOST TOWNS OF THE NORTHWEST Norman D. Weis (c) 1971 6th printing 1988 Caxton Printers, Ltd. Caldwell, ID ISBN 0-87004-201-7 319 pages Covers ghost towns in Oregon, Washington, Idaho, Wyoming and Montana. 319 pages

GHOST TOWNS OF THE WEST Lambert Florin (c) 1971 Published in 1973 by Promontry Press, New York, NY ISBN 0-88394-013-2 872 pages Covers ghost towns in Alaska, Yukon, Bristish Columbia, Arizona, California, Colorado, Utah, Montana, Idaho, Whyoming, Nevada, New Mexico, Texas, Oregon, and Washington. 872 pages

GOLD DREDGING IN SUMPTER VALLEY Brooks Hawley (c) 1977 Baker Printing and Lithography, Baker City, OR 40 pages

GOLD PANNING THE PROSPECTOR WAY Ken Alexander (c) 1979 Ken Alexander, Sumpter, OR 12 pages

GRANITE AND GOLD The Story of Oregon's Smallest City James Waucop Tabor (c) 1988 and Published by Theresa Tabor Fowler Printed by Record-Courier Printers, Baker City, OR 86 pages

HOMESTEADS AND HERITAGES: A History of Morrow County, Oregon Giles French (c) 1971 Binfords and Mort Publishers, Portland, OR ISBN 0-8323-0204-x 127 pages

MAIN STREET NORTHEASTERN OREGON The Founding and Development of Small Towns Barbara Ruth Bailey (c) 1982 The Oregon Historical Society Press Portland, OR ISBN 0-87595-073-6 220 pages

OREGON'S FADING PAST Lawrence E. Nielsen and Donald S. Galbreath (c) 1993 Maverick Publications, Inc Bend, OR ISBN 0-89288-240-9 195 pages

OREGON FIRSTS Past and Present James Andrew Long (c) 1994 Pumpkin Ridge Productions, North Plains, OR ISBN 1-882635-00-0 218 pages

OREGON GEOGRAPHIC NAMES 6TH EDITION Lewis A. McArthur, Revised by Lewis L. McArthur (c) 1992 Oregon Hisotrical Society Press, Portland, OR 958 pages

OREGON'S GOLDEN YEARS Miles F. Potter (past mayor of Greenhorn) (c) 1982 The Caxton Printers, Ltd. Caldwell, ID ISBN 0-87004-254-8 181 pages

ROADSIDE HISTORY OF OREGON Bill Gulick (c) 1991 Mountain Press Publishing, Missoula, MT ISBN 0-87842-252-8 430 pages

ROADS OF YESTERDAY IN NORTHEAST OREGON Lawrence E. Nielsen (c) 1990 Maverick Publications, Inc. Bend, OR ISBN 0-89288-805-5 143 pages

SCHOOL DAYS IN THE WALLOWAS: A History of the 91 schools and communities, past and present, of Wallowa County, Oregon Irene Locke Barklow (c) 1992 Enchantments Publishing of Oregon, Enterprise, OR & Maverick Publications, Inc. Bend, OR ISBN 0-9618185-4-9 (HB) 572 pages

SEARCH FOR OREGON'S LOST BLUE BUCKET MINE The Stephen Meek Wagon Train of 1845 Charles S. Hoffman with Bert Webber (c) 1992 Webb Researce Group, Medford, OR ISBN 0-936738-63-4 110 pages

SHANIKO From Wool Capital to Ghost Town Helen Guyton Rees (c) 1982 Binford and Mort Publishing, Portland, OR ISBN 0-8323-0399-2 Second Printing 1990 166 pages

STORIES, LEGENDS AND SOME HISTORY Carmelita Holland (c) 1996 Record Courier Printers, Baker City, OR 256 pages

THE WALLOWA COUNTRY 1867-1877 Grace Bartlett (c) 1984 Ye Galleon Press, Fairfield, WA 109 pages

UMATILLA COUNTY: A Backward Glance Umatilla County Historical Society (c) 1980 Published by E.O. Master Printers, Pendleton, OR 269 pages

NeckTie SOCIAL

POSTAL RECORDS

TOWN	POST OFFICE ESTABLISHED	POST OFFICE CLOSED
Albee	17 Apr. 1882	31 Oct. 1943
Antelope	7 Aug. 1871	still open
Ashwood	1898	?
Auburn	1 Nov. 1862	31 Oct. 1903
Bakeoven	1 Dec. 1875	1920's
Bourne	Mar. 1895	3 May 1927
Boyd	6 Mar. 1884	1960's
Cornucopia	7 Dec. 1885	June 1942
Dufur	11 Jan. 1878	still open
Flora	6 Oct. 1890	27 Dec. 1966
Friend	28 Feb. 1903	?
Galena	see Susanville	Aug. 1943
Granite	26 Mar. 1878	1957
Greenhorn	25 May 1902	15 Dec. 1919
Kent	Jan. 1887	still open
Klondike	11 Jan. 1899	30 Nov. 1951
Lonerock	Nov. 1875	1960's
McEwen	?	?
Pocahontas	4 Aug. 1863	1864 or 1872
Sherar's Bridge	1868	?
Shaniko	31 Mar. 1900	still open
Sparta	29 Oct. 1872	?
Sumpter	13 Dec. 1883	still open
Susanville	12 Sept. 1888	31 Dec. 1952
Whitney	1901	1940's
Wingville	23 June 1871	July 1879

INDEX

A

B

C

Cyanide   113

D

Dairyville   135
Dalles-California Highway   20, 33, 40
Danner   136
DeMoss   39, 133
Deschutes - Post Office   23
Diamond   136
Dog Town   135
Doodle -Bugs   90
Dufur   3, 13, 15
Durkee   134

E

Elk Creek   94, 95, 98
Elkhorn Mountains   56, 102
Enterprise   118, 121, 122
Express Ranch   134

F

Fifteenmile Creek   12, 15
Flanagan   25, 133
Flora   5, 7, 9, 118
Ford, Ote   80, 81
Fremont Power House   85
Frenchglen   136
Friend   3, 5, 8, 9, 18, 31

G

Galena   8, 94, 99
Great Southern Railroad   3, 15, 19, 31
Ghost Town - Defined   5
Ghost Town - Ettiquette   10
Goodell, Tim Wagon Train of 1862   110
Granite   5, 8, 9, 75
Greenhorn   5, 8, 85

N

O

P

R

S

T

U

W

Y

OTHER BOOKS AVAILABLE FROM DRIGH SIGHED PUBLICATIONS:

Living on the Dry Side of Oregon: Comments From the Cosmic Cowboy (c) 1997 by Keith F. May   Ever wonder what makes Eastern Oregon different from Western Oregon? Want to know how to maintain your sanity if you live in Eastern Oregon? Curious how to become a resident? Well...READ THIS humorous expose, then you can drive around Eastern Oregon and look like a native! 84 pages ISBN 1-57502-648-1 pbk $8.95

Pioneer Clothing on the Oregon Trail (c) 1998 by Christina Rae May. Ever wonder just what the pioneers wore when they travelled to Oregon? There were no zippers then, not even disposable diapers! Lots of photos and diary excerpts. 85 pages ISBN 1-57502-690-2 pbk. $10.95

A Field Guide to Historic Pendleton (c) 1997 by Keith F. May. Take a look at the origins of this once wild frontier town. Many historic homes and buildings remain to tell us about the 32 saloons and 18 bordellos of this old "Entertainment Capital of the Northwest".   180 pages ISBN 1-57502-427-6 pbk $16.95

A Field Guide to Historic The Dalles (c) 1997 by Keith F. May. Use this field guide to explore The Dalles' past as an Indian trading center, Methodist mission, Fort, site of a U.S. Mint, a rip roaring gold rush town and more. 178 pages ISBN 1-57502-446-2 pbk $15.95

Finding The Trail in Oregon: A Guide to Sites, Museums and Ruts on the Oregon Trail (c) 1996 by Keith F. May. Includes every public site of the Oregon Trail from Vale to Oregon City. 210 pages ISBN 1-57502-136-6 pbk $14.95

A Tour of Pendleton's Historic Homes (c) 1995 by Keith F. May   The history and architecture of 29 of Pendleton's historic homes. 70 pages   ISBN 1-57502-090-4 pbk $9.95

TO ORDER ANY OF THESE TITLES:

Write the titles you wish to have, along with your mailing address, and enclose a check for the total of the books ordered plus $3.00 to cover shipping and handling to:

> Drigh Sighed Publications
> 327 SE 1st Street, Suite 131
> Pendleton, OR 97801

OR:

Write to the above address to obtain a free catalog of titles available and an order form.

Keith F. May

Besides researching history and writing books, Keith is a veteran first grade teacher in Pendleton, Oregon and also an adjunct history instructor for The Heritage Institute of Seattle, Washington. He has taken hundreds of teachers out to explore the Oregon Trail and ghost towns of Eastern Oregon each summer since 1992. Keith was named "Outstanding College Educator of the Year" in 1995 by the Oregon/California Trails Association for his work teaching educators about Western Migration.

Keith was born in Pendleton and moved to The Dalles in 1956. He graduated from The Dalles High School and the University of Oregon. Keith and his wife, Christina, have also lived in Hermiston and La Grande, Oregon city and Eugene before coming home to Pendleton. They reside in an historic mansion overlooking downtown Pendleton which they are restoring to its past glory.

Keith's other works include:

Living on the Dry Side of Oregon: Comments by the Cosmic Cowboy
A Field Guide to Historic Pendleton
A Field Guide to Historic The Dalles
A Tour of Pendleton's Historic Homes
Finding The Trail in Oregon: A Guide to Sites, Museums and Ruts on the Oregon Trail